For Lang

Norwegian Grammar

by

BJARNE BERULFSEN

Dr. philos.

Professor in Norwegian at the
University of Oslo

H. ASCHEHOUG & CO. (W. NYGAARD)

OSLO 1977

On the cover:
Detail from Porch of Urnes Stave Church,
Sogn, about 1070.

Emil Moestue A.s, Oslo

ISBN 82-03-04312-7

Foreword

This grammar was published in printed form in 1963 after having gone through several stencilled editions at the International Summer School of the University of Oslo, the first of which appeared in 1957. Thanks to steadily growing interest in the study of Norwegian on the part of foreigners, both in Norway and abroad, a third impression of the printed version is now necessary. Only a few minor changes have been made in this edition.

Norway has two official written languages, viz. *bokmål (riksmål)* and *nynorsk (landsmål)*. Although the gap between the two is fairly small and is notably shrinking, the author has found it convenient to let this grammar deal with bokmål only in its most traditional form. This is in fact the idiom that the reader will encounter in the greater part of literature, newspapers, periodicals and magazines. Furthermore it comes closest to the spoken language of the majority of well-educated people, in so far as they are independent of their local, popular dialects.

The author has concentrated on the chief aspects of morphology and syntax. It has also been necessary to give an introductory view of phonetics, intonation and accent. As illustrations and examples words and phrases of comparatively high frequency are chosen. It must, however, be emphasized that the best way of obtaining mastery of spoken Norwegian is to learn it from a native teacher, either directly or indirectly by means of records, tapes in language laboratories etc.

Some Norwegian grammatical terms have been added in parenthesis after the chapter headings in order to familiarize the students with them. A few of the English translations of examples are of necessity more literal than idiomatic.

Oslo, September 1970

Bjarne Berulfsen

4. impression is an unchanged edition of 3. impression.

Oslo, January 1977

The Publisher

Page

A Short Description

OF THE PRONUNCIATION
OF THE LETTERS IN NORWEGIAN

§ 1. THE ALPHABET *(Alfabetet)*

The Norwegian alphabet consists of 29 letters. It has the same vowels as English, and in addition *æ, ø* and *å* (see § 4). The diphthongs in use are *ai, au, ei, oi (oy)* and *øy* (see § 5). The consonants are the same as in English, but *c, q, w, x* and *z* are rarely used, and then almost exclusively in foreign words that have been adopted in the form they have in the original language (see § 6).

Norwegian letters – both vowels and consonants – do not, or may not, represent quite the same sounds as far as articulation is concerned, as do the respective ones in English. When we say that a Norwegian letter has a pronunciation equivalent or nearly equivalent to the English one, the statement is approximate.

§ 2. ACCENT AND LENGTH *(Trykk og lengde)*

A syllable is either accented or unaccented. In most Norwegian words the stress is on the first syllable; emphasis on other syllables than the first usually betrays words of foreign origin: e.g. the German loanword *betale* (pay) with accented *a*, or *nasjon* (nation), which has come in from French with the stress on *o*. It should be noted that even in the least accented syllables the vowel is not silent like the "e" in English "have", "take" (see § 4 *e*).

Within the accented syllable the vowel or the consonant may be long or short. The long vowel, which is ordinarily pronounced in a more tense way than the English one, will be followed by a short, usually single consonant. The short vowel, which as a rule has a more slack or open pronunciation, will be followed by a long consonant, usually doubled (geminated). In unaccented syllables both vowels and consonants are short (see below):

> *tak* (ceiling, roof) with long *a* and short *k*
> *takk* (thank)   ”   short *a* and long *k*
> *pen* (nice)   “   long *e* and short *n*

1

penn (pen)	with short *e* and long *n*
taper (loser)	" long *a* and short *p*
tapper (brave)	" short *a* and long *p*

Both in *taper* and *tapper* the stress is on the first syllable. The ending *-er* in both words has very little stress and the *-e-* as well as the *-r* is short. If a word with a long vowel becomes the unstressed part of a compound, the vowel is pronounced only with reduced length, e.g. *kvinnehater* (women hater), but *kvinnehatter* (women's hats).

Also in front of two or more dissimilar consonants the vowel is ordinarily short: e.g. *vaske* (wash) or *disk* (counter) with short *a*, resp. *i*. A long final *m* is never doubled: e.g. *kam* (comb) with a short *a* and long *m* (see § 6 *m*). Further some small words, especially pronouns and prepositions, do not geminate the final consonant to indicate length: e.g. *han* (he), *til* (till, to), *for* (for).

§ 3.   TONES *(Tonelag)*

Norwegian words are pronounced with either single tone or double tone. In the former the melody of the word from the stressed syllable on is marked by an even rise of about six tones to the end of the word. The single tone is found in all words that are or originally were monosyllables, thus in the present tense of all strong verbs (§ 118), and also when a monosyllabic noun becomes disyllabic by the addition of the definite article (§§ 7 and 8 c):

gutt ___ (boy)   *gutt - en* (the boy) *skriv - er* (writes)

In words with double tone the melody begins a little higher, then falls about three tones and finally rises again to approximately the same height as the single tone. This is frequent in words of two or more syllables:

pi - ke (girl)

2

§ 4. VOWELS *(Vokaler)*

a

especially when long, has very much the same pronunciation as the English "a" in "father": e.g. *hat* (hate), *lage* (make), *var* (was, were), *dal* (valley). The short *a* is very similar to it also in unaccented syllables, but may be of a somewhat brighter character: e.g. *hatt* (hat), *lang* (long), *varm* (warm, hot), *falle* (fall), *hytta* (the cabin), *Europa* (Europe).

NB! *a* is never pronounced like "a" in "nation", "call", "cat", "tenant", "courage".

e

when long has a narrow pronunciation like "é" in French "café" or "ee" in German "See", which comes fairly close to the first element of the diphthongal pronunciation of the English "a" in "name" (neim). Examples are *le* (laugh), *se* (see), *ren* (clean). The short *e* in a stressed syllable corresponds well to the English "e" in "bet" or "sell": e.g. *lett* (easy), *seng* (bed).

In accented syllables the long or short *e* before *r* is frequently pronounced *æ* (see below): e.g. *her* (there), *der* (here), *er* (am, is, are). This is especially the case when the *r* is followed by another consonant: e.g. *verden* (world), *verb* (verb), *verft* (ship-yard), *Bergen* (city in West-Norway), *sterk* (strong), *perle* (pearl), *Herr* (Mr.), *vers* (verse), *vert* (host); long in *vern* (defence).

In the pronouns *de* (they), *De* (you) the *e* is pronounced like *i* (see below).

In unaccented syllables the *e* gets much the same neutral pronunciation as "e" in "garden" or "o" in "seldom": e.g. *alle* (all), *bestå* (consist), *gutten* (the boy).

The accented *é* with narrow pronunciation, and the accented *è* representing an *æ*-sound (see p. 5) appear in words that have come from French: *idé* (idea), *kupé* (compartment), *karrière* (career), *première* (first performance). The *é* in *én* (one) is sometimes used to distinguish it from the indefinite article *en* (a), cf. § 79.

In some words of French origin the *e* before *nt* is pronounced *a*: e.g. *departement* (cf. § 6 *t*).

NB! *e* is never silent like "e" in "polite", "courage" (see § 2).

i

when long is pronounced like "i" in "machine", "e" in "he", or "ee" in "see": e.g. *liv* (life), *fin* (fine), *vise* (show). The short *i* requires a bit more open articulation. Examples are *litt* (a little), *finne* (find), *trikk* (tram, streetcar). For pronunciation of *e* like *i* in *de*, *De*, see page 3.

o

both when long and frequently also when short, both in accented and unaccented syllables, has principally a narrow pronunciation that has no exact equivalent in English, representing as it does more of the "u" in German "Buch". It reminds of English "u" in "full" and English "oo" in "fool", but demands an articulation further back in the mouth and a more narrow rounding of the lips. Examples of long *o* are: *bok* (book), *mor* (mother), *skole* (school), and of short *o*: *rom* (room), *koffert* (suitcase) in accented syllables, and *lokomotiv* (locomotive), *radio* (radio) in unaccented syllables.

The short *o*-sound can also be represented by the letter *u* (see below). Very often the *o* represents an *å*-sound (see p. 5), long in *doven* (lazy), *sove* (sleep), *over* (over), and short in *holde* (keep, hold), *sommer* (summer), *opp* (up). Thus there is no difference in pronunciation between long *o* and *å* in *love* (promise), *låve* (barn), and between short *o* and *å* in *sold* (soldier's pay) and *såld* (sieve), *rotten* (the rat), and *råtten* (rotten).

NB! *o* has never diphthongal pronunciation as in English "so", "no".

u

both long and short has a more narrow and front pronunciation than the "u" in "true" or "ew" in "view", but resembles most closely these sounds. It is long in *rute* (route), *pute* (pillow), *hus* (house), *mulig* (possible), and short – in this case with a more slack articulation – in *full* (full), *sunn* (healthy), *sulten* (hungry).

Before *kk*, *ks*, *kt*, *nk*, *ng*, *m*, *ff* the *u* is often pronounced like the sound of *o* (see above): e.g. *lukke* (close, shut), *bukser* (trousers), *lukte* (smell), *dunke* (bump), *tung* (heavy), *dum* (stupid), *skuff* (drawer).

y

both long and short has the same tongue position as *i* but is articulated with very rounded lips, like the "u" in French "lune" (moon): e.g. long in *lys* (light), *ny* (new), short in *tykk* (thick), *hytte* (cabin). In *sytten* (seventeen), *syttende* (seventeenth), *sytti* (seventy), *syttiende* (seventieth) the *y* is commonly pronounced *ø* (see p. 5).

æ

is like the English "a" in "man", and is long in *bær* (berry), *være* (be), *lære* (learn, teach); short in *færre* (fewer), *lærd* (learned).
For pronunciation of *e* like *æ* see page 3.
In some words related to words with *å* the written *æ* is pronounced like long and short *e*, for instance long in *væpne* (arm) from *våpen* (arms, weapon), *forræder* (traitor) from *forråde* (betray), short in *væske* (fluid) from *våt* (wet). Also in some cases before *l* the *æ* is pronounced *e:* e.g. *hæl* (heel), *fæl* (terrible).

ø

has the same tongue position as *e*, but is articulated with very rounded lips. This pursing of the lips is tenser when the vowel is long as in *dø* (die), *brød* (bread), *løse* (solve). When the vowel is short, the pronunciation is more slack and open: *øks* (axe), *lønn* (reward, wages).

å

has a sound fairly close to the "a" in "call" or "ou" in "bought", but demands a more narrow and tense articulation. Examples of long *å* are *båt* (boat), *låne* (lend, borrow), *språk* (language), short and a little more open in *fått* (gotten), *råtten* (rotten).
For the *å*-pronunciation of words spelt with *o* see page 4.

§ 5.   DIPHTHONGS *(Diftonger)*

ai

is pronounced much like English "I" or the "y" in "by", but the Norwegian sound is quicker and more intense. Examples are *kai* (quay), *vaie* (float, wave), *hai* (shark).

au

is something like *æu* or *æv* almost as in English "how": e.g. *tau* (rope), *august* (August), *forbauset* (amazed). The same pronunciation is heard in the *eu* in some words of Greek origin: *Europa* (Europe), *terapeut* (therapist).

ei

The first element of this diphthong is an open *e* close to *æ*. Examples are *reise* (travel), *heis* (lift), *vei* (road, way), *nei* (no).

5

The same diphthongal pronunciation has *eg* before *l* and *n:* e.g. *segl* (seal), *snegl* (snail), *regn* (rain), *tegne* (draw), and also *jeg* (I), *meg* (me), *deg* (you), *seg* (himself, herself, itself, themselves), and *-ek-* in *seksten* (sixteen), *sekstende* (sixteenth); cf. § 6 *k*.

oi (oy)

The narrow *o* in this diphthong is found only in the interjection *hoi* (ho!) and the corresponding verb *hoie* (shout ho). In other cases the pronunciation is more like English "oy" in "boy": e.g. *konvoi* (convoy), and spelt as in English: *soyabønne* (Soya bean).

øy

is composed of an open *ø* and something between a slack *y* and a rounded *i:* *øy* (island), *høy* (high), *fornøyelse* (pleasure).
The same diphthongal pronunciation is found in *øg* before *n:* e.g. *døgn* (24 hours), *løgn* (lie); cf. § 6 *g*.

§ 6. CONSONANTS *(Konsonanter)*

b

is like the English b: *bad* (bath), *blåse* (blow), *hybel* (den, digs), long in *jobb* (job), *kobber* (copper).

c

occurs only in foreign words and is pronounced *s* before *e, i, y,* for instance *cent* (cent), *cirka* (about), *cyanamid* (cyanamide), *scene* (scene, stage). In most cases such words are now spelt with *s,* for instance *sement* (cement), *sigarett* (cigarette), *sypress* (cypress).
The combination of *ch* before vowels gives a sh-sound: e.g. *champagne* (champagne), but is mostly replaced by the spelling *sj:* e.g. *sjekk* (cheque), *marsj* (march).
In all other cases *c* is pronounced like *k:* e.g. *cocktail, back, camping, corner* with English pronunciation. The *c* is, however, in similar positions mostly superseded by *k:* e.g. *koks* (cokes), *sjokk* (shock).

d

is pronounced like the English "d": *dag* (day), *drikke* (drink), *bade* (bathe, swim), long in *padde* (toad).
The *d* is often silent at the end of a word after a vowel, between vowels, and usually after *r:* e.g. *god* (good), *glad* (glad), *blad* (leaf, news-

6

paper), *slede* (sled), *jord* (earth), *fjord* (fiord, firth). Chief exceptions
are *Gud* (God), *nåde* (grace), *bad* (bath), *bade* (bathe), *ed* (oath),
mord (murder), *lærd* (learned), *verden* (world), *verdi* (value), where
the *d* is heard.

After *l* and *n* the *d* is frequently assimilated to the pronunciation *ll*
and *nn*: *kald* (cold), *holde* (hold, keep), *vind* (wind), *land* (land,
country), *blande* (mix). Some exceptions are *alder* (age), *skulder*
(shoulder), *handel* (trade), *kunde* (customer), where the *d* is heard.
Furthermore the *d* is pronounced before derivative syllables; thus
not heard in *ende* (end), but pronounced in *endelig* (finally), silent in
blod (blood), but pronounced in *blodig* (bloody). Before *t* the *d* is
assimilated to *tt*: *midte* (middle).

f

sounds like English "f" or like "gh" in "enough": *far* (father), *falle*
(fall), long in *stoff* (material), *gaffel* (fork).

The *ph* is seldom used for *f*, see *p* page 9.

g

is pronounced hard like English "g" in "good", "dog" in most cases:
e.g. *gate* (street), *gull* (gold), *lage* (make), *ligge* (lie), *Norge* (Norway).
Before a *j* the *g* is not pronounced at all: e.g. *gjøre* (do), *gjespe*
(yawn) (see *j* p. 8), but it is not silent before *n* as in English: *gnage*
(gnaw), *gni* (rub); cf. *k* p. 8. Before *i, y, ei* the letter has the same
pronunciation as the Norwegian *j* (see p. 8), e.g. *gi* (give), *begynne*
(begin), *geit* (goat), but is hard in foreign words like *gitar* (guitar),
gymnasium (grammar school, high school).

As for diphthongal pronunciation of *eg* and *øg*, see § 5 *ei* and *øy*.
In the adjective suffix *-ig* the *g* is always silent: e.g. *heldig* (lucky),
rolig (quiet), but it is usually hardened to a *k*-sound before *s* in the
superlative (cf. § 62): *roligst* (most quiet). The *g* is also silent in *deig*
(dough), *haug* (mound), *og* (and).

In some words the combination of *l* and *g* is assimilated to the
pronunciation *ll*: e.g. *følge* (accompany, follow), *selge* (sell), but
not in *bølge* (wave), *følge* (consequence), *selger* (seller).

The *g* is silent in *morgen* (morning) and assimilated to *rr* in *i morges*
(this morning).

The English pronunciation is adopted in the loanwords *gin, gentleman*,
whereas *g* in the French loan-words *geni* (genius) and the adjective
generell (general) is sounded "sh".

The combination *ng* in the end of a word has the pronunciation of
"ng" in the same position in English words: e.g. *lang* (long), *ting*

7

(thing), but this sound is preserved also when a vowel is added: e.g. *mange* (many) and is not followed by a hard g-sound as in English "finger".

The combination *gn* is usually pronounced as *ngn:* e.g. in *vogn* (wagon), *gagn* (advantage), *ligne* (resemble).

For the pronunciation *ng* in words of French origin spelt *nt*, see *t* page 10.

h

before vowels has the sound of English "h" in "he", "hope": e.g. *han* (he), *håpe* (hope), *beholde* (keep). It is not heard before *j:* e.g. *hjelpe* (help), *hjul* (wheel), *hjørne* (corner). It is also silent in the combination *hv*, which often corresponds to English "wh": e.g. *hvem* (who), *hval* (whale), *hvete* (wheat), *hvit* (white).

j

is pronounced like the opening sound in "yes" or "yawn": e.g. *ja* (yes), *jul* (Christmas), *linje* (line).

A few words borrowed from English have sometimes kept up the English pronunciation: e.g. *jeep*, whereas *jet* (plane) is sounded like "yet".

k

is much the same as "k" in English: e.g. *kake* (cake), *krig* (war), long in *vakker* (beautiful). **It is not silent before** *n: knytte* (tie); cf. *g* page 7.

In connection with *j* the *k* becomes a voiceless sound, made more fricative than the opening sound in English "hue" by raising the middle of the tongue towards the palate so as to produce a very narrow passage; cf. *t* p. 10. Examples are *kjøre* (drive), *kjeller* (cellar), *kjær* (dear).

The same pronunciation has *k* in front of *i, y, ei:* e.g. *kino* (cinema), *kirke* (church), *kyst* (coast), *kei* (bored). But the hard *k* is heard in the loan-words *kippers* (kippers), *arkiv* (archive), *kynisk* (cynical), *keiser* (emperor).

The *-ek-* in *seksten* (sixteen) and *sekstende* (sixteenth) becomes a diphthong *ei;* see § 5.

l

has about the same sound as in English "land", "flat". Examples are *liten* (little), *le* (laugh), *flagg* (flag). Norwegian *l* has not the hollow pronunciation of the "l" in English "tall", "full" but is articulated with the tongue against the inner edge of the upper teeth: *falle* (fall), *tall* (number).

The *l* is silent before *j*: e.g. in *ljå* (scythe), *ljome* (resound, echo).

m

is like English "m": e.g. *mat* (food), *dame* (lady), long in *komme* (come). The long *m* in the end of a word is never doubled: e.g. *dum* (stupid), *dom* (judgement), *lam* (lamb), but it is geminated when the word gets an inflective ending beginning with a vowel: e.g. *dummere* (more stupid), *dommen* (the judgement), *lammet* (the lamb); cf. §§ 10, 14, 46, 62.

n

is like English "n": e.g. *nå* (now), *natt* (night), *snø* (snow), long in *tann* (tooth). Before *g* and *k* the *n* sounds as it does in English: *lang* (long), *bank* (bank); cf. *g* page 7.

In the suffix *-anse*, which has come from French, the pronunciation becomes *-angse: korrespondanse* (correspondence).

p

is like English "p" in for instance *penn* (pen), *plikt* (duty), *skarp* (sharp), long in *stoppe* (stop).

The combination *ph* never occurs in Norwegian words, and is replaced by *f* (see p. 7) in loan-words as well: e.g. *filosofi* (philosophy), *diftong* (diphthong). It will, however, be found in academic titles like *dr. philos.*, i.e. *doctor philosophiae* (doctor of philosophy).

q

appears only in loan-words that have been adopted in their foreign form: e.g. *quick-step*. The combination *qu* is replaced by *kv*, for instance *kvartett* (quartet), *kvalifikasjon* (qualification).

r

has a varied pronunciation in Norway. Advisable is an imitation of the trilled consonant heard in Scotland: e.g. in *rot* (root), *herre* (gentleman). It will facilitate the understanding if it is always pronounced very distinctly, even before *d, n, l, t*, where it tends to get a thicker pronunciation although not so much as in American. The combination *rs* will often result in a sh-sound: e.g. *verst* (worst), *mars* (March).

NB! Take care to pronounce the *r* very clearly at the end of syllables stressed or unstressed, where it is not heard in English: e.g. *for* (for), *doktor* (doctor), *finger* (finger).

s

corresponds to the English "s" in words like "song", "less" and the "c" in "fence". Examples are *synge* (sing), *lese* (read), *skole* (school), *seks* (six), long in *kasse* (case). The *s* is never voiced as in English "has", "rise".

The combination *sj* is pronounced like English "sh": e.g. *sjel* (soul), *sjø* (sea). The same pronunciation applies to *skj*, for instance in *skjorte* (shirt), *skjørt* (skirt), and *sk* before *i, y, ei, øy:* e.g. *ski* (ski), *skyte* (shoot), *skeie ut* (take to a dissolute life), *skøyte* (skate). The combination *sh* is found only in some loan-words: e.g. *shilling* (the earlier Norwegian coin of the same name spelt *skilling*) and *sch*, pronounced similarly, in *backfisch* (flapper).

t

is much the same as in English: *tale* (speak), *gate* (street), long in *katt* (cat), *sitte* (sit).

The combination *th*, which may occur in foreign words and in some proper names, stands for "t" as in "Thames", not the "th" in "think", "that".

tj has exactly the same pronunciation as *kj* (see p. 8): e.g. *tjære* (tar), *tjern* (little lake). Exceptions: *tjene* (serve), *tjeneste* (service). *t* is silent in the pronoun *det* (it, that, the) and also in the definite form of neutral nouns: e.g. *landet* (the country). But it is usually heard when followed by a genitive *s:* e.g. *landets* (the country's); cf. § 26.

In some words of French origin the *nt* has the pronunciation of *ng:* e.g. *interessant* (interesting), *departement* (department); cf. § 4 *e.*

v

may be compared to the English "v", but it is less fricative: e.g. *vår* (spring), *love* (promise), *hav* (ocean).

In some words the combination of *l* and *v* is assimilated to *ll:* e.g. in *halv* (half), *sølv* (silver), *tolv* (twelve), but not in *kalv* (calf), *skjelve* (shiver), *elv* (river).

10

occurs only in some loan-words adopted in their original form: e.g. *whisky, show, week-end*. It is pronounced like *v*, by which it is often replaced, for instance *vel* (well).

x

is found only in some words of foreign origin and form, and is pronounced *ks:* e.g. *foxtrot*, and in front position *s: xylograf* (xylograph). It is mostly replaced by *ks* in spelling too: e.g. *ortodoks* (orthodox), *eksamen* (examination).

z

is used in some foreign words, and the pronunciation is like *s*. Examples are *zoologi* (zoology), *zeppeliner* (zeppelin), *razzia* (razzia).

Nouns *(Substantiver)*

GENDER AND NUMBER *(Kjønn og tall)*

SINGULAR *(Entall)*

§ 7. **There are three genders in Norwegian.**

	Indefinite form *(Ubestemt form)*	Definite form *(Bestemt form)*
a) **Masculine** *(hankjønn)* or *en*-gender:	*en gutt* (a boy)	*gutten* (the boy)
b) **Feminine** *(hunkjønn)* or *a*-gender:	*en* or *ei ku* (a cow)	*kua* (the cow)
c) **Neuter** *(intetkjønn)* or *et*-gender	*et hus* (a house)	*huset* (the house)

§ 8. a) The words *en, ei, et*, corresponding to English "a" ("an"), are the indefinite articles.

b) **The indefinite article** *(ubestemt artikkel)* **of a masculine is *en*, of a feminine *en* or *ei*, of a neuter *et*.**

c) The definite article *(bestemt artikkel)*, corresponding to "the", is post-positive, i.e. placed at the end of the noun. In masculine it is *-en (gutten)*, in feminine *-a (kua)*, in neuter *-et (huset)*, where the *t* is silent (cf. § 6 *t*). Nouns of two or more syllables, ending in an unstressed *-e* in the indefinite form, get only *-n* in the definite form masculine and *-t* in the definite form neuter*. In the definite form feminine *-e* is changed into *-a*.

en pakke (a packet)	– *pakken* (the packet)
et stykke (a piece)	– *stykket* (the piece)
en or *ei hytte* (a cabin)	– *hytta* (the cabin)

d) Many nouns may use either definite article, *-en* or *-a*, i.e. they may be either masculine or feminine. Such words are:

en (ei) kasse (a case)	– *kassen* or *kassa* (the case)
ein (ei) tid (a time)	– *tiden* or *tida* (the time)

§ 9. For a long period the bokmål had only two grammatical genders, the original feminine having coalesced with the masculine into a common gender *(felleskjønn)* using *-en* as definite article. Through the spelling reforms of 1917 and 1938 and the text-book norm of 1959 a full system of three genders was provided for, but there are still comparatively few nouns that are obligatorily feminine or *a*-gender. Readers of bokmål (riksmål) literature in fiction, scientific publications, periodicals, magazines, and newspapers will mainly encounter just two genders, common and neuter. In order to simplify matters, we shall in this grammar mostly refer to the nouns as being either common (*en*-nouns) or neuter (*et*-nouns) taking respectively *en* or *et* as indefinite articles.

§ 10. As mentioned above (§§ 2 and 6 *m*) a long *m*-sound at the end of a word is not geminated. But we double the *m* when the definite article is added, also when the noun becomes the unstressed second part of a compound: *dom* (sentence) – *dommen* (the sentence), *dødsdom* (death sentence) – *dødsdommen* (the death sentence), *hjem* (home) – *hjemmet* (the home), *gamlehjem* (old people's home) – *gamlehjemmet* (the old people's home). This gemination is also found in nouns with the suffix *-dom: ungdom* (youth) – *ungdommen* (the youth). The same doubling of the *m* in the plural (§ 14).

---

*) Words ending in a stressed *-e* (or *-é*) take the full ending *-en* or *-et* in the definite form: e.g. *en skje* (spoon) – *skjeen* (the spoon), *et kne* (a knee) – *kneet* (the knee), *en idé* (an idea) – *idéen* (the idea), *et palé* (a palace) – *paléet* (the palace).

12

§ 11. Neuters ending in unstressed -el, -der and -ter can drop the e before l and r in the definite form. In case a double consonant collides with the l and r, it is reduced to a single one:

et fengsel (a prison)	– fengselet or fengslet (the prison)
et bissel (a bridle)	– bisselet or bislet (the bridle)
et under (a wonder)	– underet or undret (the wonder)
et sludder (a nonsense)	– sludderet or sludret (the nonsense)
et teater (a theatre)	– teateret or teatret (the theatre)
et gitter (a grate)	– gitteret or gitret (the grate)

§ 12. Some foreign words in Latin form have an irregular definite form (also plural, see § 23):

en radius (a radius)   – radien (the radius)

Note particularly a group of neuters ending in -um or -ium:

et verbum (a verb)*	– verbet (the verb)
et sentrum (a center)*	– sentret (the center)
et museum (a museum)	– museet (the museum)
et gymnasium (a grammar school, a high school)*	– gymnasiet (the grammar school, the high school)
et stipendium (a scholarship)*	– stipendiet (the scholarship)
et evangelium (a gospel)	– evangeliet (the gospel)
et laboratorium (a laboratory)	– laboratoriet (the laboratory)

PLURAL (Flertall)

§ 13. **By far the greater part of the nouns take the ending -er in the plural indefinite form and -ene in the definite form plural. If the noun consists of two or more syllables ending in an unstressed -e, the respective plural endings are just -r and -ne.** The stressed -e or -é takes full ending -er and -ene. Cf. § 8 c and note.

en gutt (a boy)	– gutter (boys)	– guttene (the boys)
en or ei ku (a cow)	– kuer (cows)	– kuene (the cows); cf. § 19 b.
et sted (a place)	– steder (places)	– stedene (the places)
en sofa (a sofa)	– sofaer (sofas)	– sofaene (the sofas)

*) The irregularity about these nouns has led to the forming of reduced indefinite forms singular, respectively et verb, et senter, et gymnas, et stipend.

13

skje (spoon)	– *skjeer* (spoons)	– *skjeene* (the spoons)
en idé (an idea)	– *idéer* (ideas)	– *idéene* (the ideas)
et palé (a palace)	– *paléer* (palaces)	– *paléene* (the palaces)
en time (an hour)	– *timer* (hours)	– *timene* (the hours)
en (ei) hytte (a cabin)	– *hytter* (cabins)	– *hyttene* (the cabins)
et værelse (a room)	– *værelser* (rooms)	– *værelsene* (the rooms)

§ 14. With gemination of the final *m;* cf. § 10:

en drøm (a dream)	– *drømmer* (dreams)	– *drømmene* (the dreams)
en ungdom (a youth)	– *ungdommer* (young people)	– *ungdommene* (the young people)
et medlem (a member)	– *medlemmer* (members)	– *medlemmene* (the members)

§ 15. **Most monosyllabic neuters have no ending in the indefinite form plural, but -*ene* in the definite form plural:**

et år (a year)	– *år* (years)	– *årene* (the years)
et ord (a word)	– *ord* (words)	– *ordene* (the words)
et land (a country)	– *land* (countries)	– *landene* (the countries)
et brød (a loaf of bread)	– *brød* (loaves of bread)	– *brødene* (the loaves of bread)

This is also the case with such neuters forming part of a compound:

et skuddår (a leapyear)	– *skuddår* (leapyears)	– *skuddårene* (the leapyears)
et skjellsord (an abusive word)	– *skjellsord* (abusive words)	– *skjellsordene* (the abusive words)
et fedreland (a native country)	– *fedreland* (native countries)	– *fedrelandene* (the native countries)
et rugbrød (a loaf of rye bread)	– *rugbrød* (loaves of rye bread)	– *rugbrødene* (the loaves of rye bread)

§ 16. In literature as well as in spoken language some monosyllabic neuters, especially loan-words, may also be given the ending -*er* in the indefinite plural:

| *et kart* (a map) | – *kart(er)* (maps) | – *kartene* (the maps) |
| *et brev* (a letter) | – *brev(er)* (letters) | – *brevene* (the letters) |

14

NB! Always:

et sted (a place)	– *steder* (places)	– *stedene* (the places)
et lem (a limb)	– *lemmer* (limbs)	– *lemmene* (the limbs)

IRREGULAR PLURAL *(Uregelmessig flertall)*

§ 17. Nouns ending in unaccented *-el*, drop the *-e-* in the indefinite and definite plural, and a previous double consonant is then reduced to a single one. The same thing happens to nouns ending in unaccented *-er* (cp. § 18), but here the indefinite plural of *et*-nouns is formed by adding just *-e* or it takes no ending at all:

en støvel (a boot)	– *støvler* (boots)	– *støvlene* (the boots)
et eksempel (an example)	– *eksempler* (examples)	– *eksemplene* (the examples)
en sykkel (a cycle)	– *sykler* (cycles)	– *syklene* (the cycles)
et bissel (a bridle)	– *bisler* (bridles)	– *bislene* (the bridles)
en vinter (a winter)	– *vintrer* (winters)	– *vintrene* (the winters)
en sommer (a summer)	– *somrer* (summers)	– *somrene* (the summers)
et orkester (an orchestra)	– *orkestre* or *orkester* (orchestras)	– *orkestrene* (the orchestras)
et gitter (a grate)	– *gitre* or *gitter* (grates)	– *gitrene* (the grates)

See also § 21.

§ 18. *En*-**nouns ending in unstressed** *-er* **and denoting profession or nationality, take only** *-e* **in the indefinite plural and** *-ne* **(not** *-ene*) **in the definite plural:**

lærer (teacher)	– *lærere* (teachers)	– *lærer**ne** (the teachers)
amerikaner (American)	– *amerikaner**e*** (Americans)	– *amerikaner**ne** (the Americans)*

§ 19. The following monosyllabic *en*-nouns (also as the last part of compounds) form their plural by changing the vowel, *å* into *æ*, *a* into *e*, *o* into *ø*, and *u* into *y*.

*) Note that names of nationalities are **not** capitalized in Norwegian; cf. § 44 b, note **.

15

a) plural endings *-er, -ene:*

1)

and (duck)	– *ender* (ducks)	– *endene* (the ducks)
hand or *hånd* (hand)	– *hender* (hands)	– *hendene* (the hands)
kraft (power, strength) (also *hestekraft* [horsepower])	– *krefter*	– *kreftene*
mark (half a pound)	– *merker*	– *merkene*
natt (night)	– *netter*	– *nettene*
rand (stripe, edge, margin)	– *render*	– *rendene*
stang (bar, pole, rod) (also *fiskestang* [fishing rod])	– *stenger*	– *stengene*
stand (social class)	– *stender*	– *stendene*
strand (beach)	– *strender*	– *strendene*
tang (tongs, forceps)	– *tenger*	– *tengene*
tann (tooth)	– *tenner*	– *tennene*
stad (town, city) (also *hovedstad* [capital])	– *steder*	– *stedene*
bok (book)	– *bøker*	– *bøkene*
bot (patch, fine)	– *bøter*	– *bøtene*
not (seine, sweep-net)	– *nøter*	– *nøtene*

2) Likewise the following disyllabic noun:

bonde (farmer)	– *bønder*	– *bøndene*

3) Insertion of *j* in:

skåk (shaft of sleigh or carriage)	– *skjæker*	– *skjækene*

4) With doubling of the consonant:

fot (foot)	– *føtter*	– *føttene*
rot (root)	– *røtter*	– *røttene*

b) with the respective endings *-r, -rne:*

glo (glow)	– *glør*	– *glørne*
klo (claw)	– *klør*	– *klørne*

16

ku (cow)	– *kyr*	– *kyrne;* but also regular; cf. § 13.
rå (ship's yard)	– *rær*	– *rærne*
tå (toe)	– *tær*	– *tærne*

c) no ending in the indefinite plural and *-ene* in the definite plural:

| *gås* (goose) | – *gjess* | – *gjessene* |
| *mann* (man) | – *menn* | – *mennene* |

§ 20. Some *en*-nouns, particularly those indicating measure or value, have no ending in the indefinite plural, and some of them just *-ne* in the definite form:

meter (metre)	– *meter*	– *meterne*
liter (litre)	– *liter*	– *literne*
øre (1/100 krone)	– *øre*	– *ørene*
fot (foot)	– *fot*	– *fotene*
mil (10 kilometers)	– *mil*	– *milene*
mann (man)	– *mann*****	

NB!
ting (thing)	– *ting*	– *tingene*
feil (mistake)	– *feil*	– *feilene*
mus (mouse)	– *mus*	– *musene*
lus (louse)	– *lus*	– *lusene*
sko (shoe)	– *sko* or *skor*	– *skoene* or *skorne*
ski (ski)	– *ski* or *skier*	– *skiene*

§ 21. Note the following nouns for relationship:

far (father)	– *fedre*	– *fedrene*
mor (mother)	– *mødre* or *mødrer*	– *mødrene*
bror (brother)	– *brødre*	– *brødrene*
søster (sister)	– *søstre* or *søstrer*	– *søstrene*
datter (daughter)	– *døtre* or *døtrer*	– *døtrene*

See also § 17.

With no singular:
| | – *søsken* brother(s) and sister(s) | – *søskenene* |
| | – *foreldre* (parents) | – *foreldrene* |

§ 22. The following neuters have irregular formation of plural:

klede (cloth)   – *klær* (clothes)   – *klærne* (the clothes)
(In compounds the singular form is just *-kle:* e.g. *håndkle* (towel), *tørkle* (scarf), *forkle* (apron), but in the plural *-klær, -klærne*.)

*) For instance: *en flokk på ti mann* (a flock of ten men).

tre (tree)	– *trær*	– *trærne*
kne (knee)	– *knær*	– *knærne*
øye (eye)	– *øyne* or *øyer*	– *øynene* or *øyene*

§ 23. Some foreign words have irregular plural:

a) *En*-nouns:

| *en kollega* (a colleague) | – *kolleger* (colleagues) | – *kollegene* (the colleagues) |
| *en radius* (a radius) | – *radier* (radii) | – *radiene* (the radii); cf. § 12 |

b) *Et*-nouns; cf. § 12:

kursus or *kurs* (course)	– *kurser*	– *kursene*
evangelium (gospel)	– *evangelier*	– *evangeliene*
sentrum (center)	– *sentrer*	– *sentrene*
verbum (verb)	– *verber* or *verb*	– *verbene*
museum (museum)	– *museer*	– *museene*

With regard to the indefinite singular forms *gymnas, verb*, see § 12 note.

c) A few neuter loan-words form their indefinite plural in the same way as the original language:

leksikon (encyclopedia, dictionary) – *leksika* (or *leksikoner*), *faktum* (fact) – *fakta, pensum* (curriculum) – *pensa, aktivum* (asset) – *aktiva* (or *aktiver*), *passivum* (liability) – *passiva* (or *passiver*).

§ 24. Since 1938 the ending *-a* in the definite plural has been obligatory for a few neuters. The most frequent representative is:

et barn (a child)   – *barn* (children)   – *barna* (the children)

This formation of definite plural can in fact be applied to most neuters ending in a consonant: e.g. *hus* (house), *brev* (letter), *skip* (ship) etc. However, those who study Norwegian through newspapers, magazines etc., will seldom encounter it.

CASES *(Kasus)*

§ 25. Norwegian has only two cases, nominative and genitive. The nominative form is also used as object, indirect object and when governed by prepositions.

GENITIVE *(Genitiv)*

§ 26. **The genitive is formed by adding *-s* to the nominative both in the indefinite and definite form, singular and plural:**

en manns	– *mannens*	– *menns*	– *mennenes*
(a man's)	(the man's)	(men's)	(the men's)
en konges	– *kongens*	– *kongers*	– *kongenes*
(a king's)	(the king's)	(kings')	(the kings')

Examples: *en times søvn* (an hour's sleep), *en ukes tid* (one week's time), *Ibsens dramaer* (Ibsen's dramas), *barnets foreldre* (the child's parents), *barnas foreldre* (the children's parents), *flere dagers arbeid* (several days' work). As will be seen from these examples, the genitive case takes no apostrophe. This is only applied in nouns already ending in *-s:* e.g. *Kong Hans's regjering* (King Hans's reign).

§ 27. There is a tendency in Norwegian to replace the *s*-genitive by prepositional expressions, as is done in English. Instead of saying *guttens far* (the child's father), *husets eier* (the house's owner), *flere dagers arbeid* (several days' work), *ved månedens slutt* (at the month's end), *Norges konge* (Norway's king) we often say *far til gutten* (father of the boy), *eieren av huset* (the owner of the house), *arbeid for flere dager* (work for several days), *ved slutten av måneden* (at the end of the month), *kongen av Norge* (the king of Norway). Sometimes compounds may be preferable: *fjelltoppen* (the mountain top) instead of *fjellets topp* (the mountain's top), *skolebarna* (the school children) instead of *skolens barn* (the school's children), *lyshastigheten* (the velocity of light) instead of *lysets hastighet* (the light's velocity).

§ 28. In foreign proper names the foreign genitive is sometimes used: e.g. *Jesu liv* (the life of Jesus), *Columbi egg* (Columbi egg). In the Bible the names of the writers of gospels are expressed without any genitive *-s* at all: *Matteus evangelium, Markus evangelium, Lukas evangelium, Johannes evangelium.*

§ 29. Unlike English the genitive case is not used in the following instances: *Vi kjøper sukker hos kolonialkjøpmannen* (we buy sugar at the grocer's) *Jeg bor hos min bror* (I live at my brother's) *Jeg er en venn av hans bror* (I am a friend of his brother's)

§ 30. In some standard phrases the genitive is used after the preposition *til: til fjells* (to the mountains, up in the mountains), *til sjøs* (to sea, at sea), *til lands* (on land), *til sengs* (to bed), *til bords* (to the table, at the table), *til fots* (on foot). Cp. § 150, *til.*

SOME RULES ABOUT GENDERS IN NORWEGIAN

§ 31. English-speaking students, being unaccustomed to nouns of different gender will naturally find it difficult to decide whether Norwegian nouns are masculine, feminine (*en*-nouns) or neuter (*et*-nouns). The best thing to do is to consult an ordinary vocabulary for Norwegians. To some extent, however, the gender can be determined according to meaning and to form.

§ 32. *En*-nouns according to meaning:

a) Nouns denoting divine and human beings, persons, animals, birds, fishes, insects etc.: *gud* (god), *engel* (angel), *djevel* (devil), *mann* (man), *kvinne* (woman), *gutt* (boy), *pike* (girl), *sønn* (son), *datter* (daughter), *lege* (doctor), *lærer* (teacher), *kelner* (waiter), *sjåfør* (driver), *hest* (horse), *hund* (dog), *katt* (cat), *gris* (pig), *fugl* (bird), *svale* (swallow), *torsk* (cod), *laks* (salmon), *flue* (fly), *mygg* (mosquito), *veps* (wasp).
Chief exceptions: Some nouns comprising both sexes are neuters: e.g. *folk* (people), *barn* (child), *vesen* (being), *menneske* (person), *troll* (troll), *bud* (messenger), *dyr* (animal), *fe* (cattle), *svin* (pig). The following nouns for female beings are mostly used as feminines: *budeie* (milk-maid), *jente* (girl), *kjerring* (woman), *møy* (virgin), *bikkje* (dog), *geit* (goat), *ku* (cow).

b) Trees, plants, fruits and parts of them: *gran* (spruce), *furu* (fir), *bjørk* (birch), *eik* (oak), *plante* (plant), *tomat* (tomato), *pære* (pear), *frukt* (fruit), *hvete* (wheat), *drue* (grape), *nøtt* (nut), *blomst* (flower), *kål* (cabbage), *rot* (root), *stamme* (stem), *grein* (branch), *kvist* (twig), *knopp* (bud), *kjerne* (core).
Neuters are: *tre* (tree), *strå* (straw), *korn* (grain), *bygg* (barley), *bær* (berry), *blad* (leaf), *eple* (apple), *frø* (seed), *skall* (peel).

c) Stones:
stein (stone), *malm* (ore), *flint* (flint), *granitt* (granite).

d) Nouns for topography, scenery, landscape, rivers, lakes:
jord (earth), *mark* (field), *slette* (plain), *skog* (wood), *dal* (valley), *fjord* (fiord), *åker* (corn-field), *øy* (island), *elv* (river), *bekk* (brook), *vik* (bay), *bre* (glacier), *høyde* (height), *sjø* (lake), *dam* (dam).
Neuters are: *sund* (sound), *tjern* (lakelet), *vann* (water), *hav* (ocean), *land* (land, country), *fjell* (mountain).

e) Climate and meteorology:
vind (wind), *storm* (storm), *bris* (breeze), *skur* (shower), *tåke* (fog), *snø* (snow), *is* (ice), *torden* (thunder), *dugg* (dew), *sky* (cloud).
Neuters are: *vær* (weather), *regn* (rain), *hagl* (hail), *klima* (climate).

f) Seasons, divisions of time, astronomy:
sommer (summer), *vår* (spring), *dag* (day), *natt* (night), *måned* (month), *uke* (week), *time* (hour), *tid* (time), *stund* (while), *jul* (Christmas), *påske* (Easter), *sol* (sun), *måne* (moon), *stjerne* (star), *himmel* (sky).
Neuters are: *år* (year), *døgn* (day and night, i. e. 24 hours), *kvartal* (3 months), *sekund* (second), *minutt* (minute), *øyeblikk* (moment).

g) Names of sciences and subjects:
vitenskap (science), *fysikk* (physics), *sosiologi* (sociology), *jus* (law), *stenografi* (stenography).

h) Names of parts of the bodies of human beings and animals:
kropp (body), *panne* (forehead), *nese* (nose), *rygg* (back), *mave* (stomach), *arm* (arm), *hånd* (hand), *legg* (calf), *fot* (foot), *hale* (tail), *snabel* (trunk).
Neuters: *legeme* (body), *hår* (hair), *øye* (eye), *øre* (ear), *bryst* (breast), *ben* (leg), *horn* (horn).

i) Names of tools and implements:
hammer (hammer), *tang* (tongs), *sag* (saw), *skje* (spoon), *kniv* (knife), *gaffel* (fork), *kam* (comb).
Neuters: *spett* (bar), *bor* (bore, drill).

§ 33. Neuters according to meaning are:

a) Names of metals:
metall (metal), *gull* (gold), *sølv* (silver), *kobber* (copper), *jern* (iron), *bly* (lead), *tinn* (tin), *stål* (steel).
En-nouns are: *malm* (ore), *messing* (brass), *sink* (zink), *bronse* (bronze), *nikkel* (nickel).

b) Substances:
vann (water), *kull* (coal), *salt* (salt), *flesk* (pork), *kjøtt* (meat), *blod* (blood), *lær* (leather), *papir* (paper), *smør* (butter), *brød* (bread), *øl* (beer), *sukker* (sugar).
En-nouns are: *melk* (milk), *fløte* (cream), *olje* (oil), *te* (tea), *kaffe* (coffee).

c) Collective nouns:
fe (cattle), *gras* or *gress* (grass), *høy* (hay), *lauv* or *løv* (leaf), *gryn* (cereal), *mel* (flour), *korn* (grain, corn), *hår* (hair), *skjegg* (beard).

§ 34. *En*-nouns according to form:

a) Nouns with the following suffixes:
-dom: barndom (childhood), *rikdom* (wealth)
-ed: måned (month). Neuter: *herred* (district)

21

-else: hendelse (event), *øvelse* (exercise). Neuters: *værelse* (room), *spøkelse* (ghost)
-er: hammer (hammer), *viser* (hand, on watch)
-het: kjærlighet (love), *frihet* (freedom)
-ing: bygning (building), *stilling* (position)
-inne: lærerinne (woman teacher), *skuespillerinne* (actress)
-nad: søknad (application), *bunad* (national costume)
-sel: redsel (fear), *ferdsel* (traffic). Neuter: *fengsel* (prison)

b) Foreign words with the following suffixes:
-a: villa (villa), *sofa* (sofa); (cp. § 35 c)
-ade: sjokolade (chocolate), *marmelade* (marmalade)
-ale: skandale (scandal), *finale* (finale)
-alje: medalje (medal), *batalje* (battle)
-ans: substans (substance), *pregnans* (brevity)
-anse: eleganse (elegance), *korrespondanse* (correspondence)
-ant: emigrant (emigrant), *hydrant* (hydrant)
-asje: etasje (floor), *garasje* (garage)
-at: granat (grenade), *termostat* (thermostat)
-att: debatt (debate), *rabatt* (discount)
-é: kafé (café), *idé* (idea)
-ens: konsekvens (consequence), *intelligens* (intelligence)
-ett: billett (ticket), *rakett* (rocket)
-fon: telefon (telephone), *grammofon* (gramophone)
-graf: telegraf (telegraph), *autograf* (autograph)
-i: energi (energy), *koloni* (colony)
-ikk: fabrikk (factory), *panikk* (panic)
-isme: patriotisme (patriotism), *kommunisme* (communism)
-log: monolog (monologue), *dialog* (dialogue)
-ong: medaljong (medallion), *fasong* (shape)
-or: motor (motor), *transformator* (transformer)
-sis: basis (basis), *krisis* (crisis)
-sjon: stasjon (station), *nasjon* (nation)
-tet: kvalitet (quality), *aktivitet* (activity)
-ur: natur (nature), *kultur* (culture)
-us: status (status), *kasus* (case)
-ør: parlør (phrase book), *vigør* (vigour)

Neuters are: *pensjonat* (boarding house), *resultat* (result), *toalett* (toilet), *diktatur* (dictatorship), *kreatur* (creature), *humør* (humour).

§ 35. *Et*-words according to form:

a) Nouns having the same form as the stem of the verb, i. e. infinitive minus the unstressed -e (cf. § 113), are often neuters:

et bad (a bath) from *bade* (to bathe), *et råd* (advice) from *råde* (advise), *et besøk* (a visit) from *besøke* (to visit), *et kjøp* (a purchase) from *kjøpe* (to purchase, buy), *et kall* (a call) from *å kalle* (to call), *et kast* (a throw) from *å kaste* (to throw).

b) Nouns with the following suffixes:
-*dømme: kongedømme* (kingdom), *bispedømme* (bishopric)
-*ende: vitende* (knowledge), *tilgodehavende* (account)
-*eri: meieri* (dairy), *maleri* (painting)
-*mål: slagsmål* (fighting), *spørsmål* (question)
-*skap: vennskap* (friendship), *fiendskap* (enmity)
En-nouns are: *kunnskap* (knowledge), *vitenskap* (science).

c) Foreign words with the following suffixes:
-*a* (in words of Greek origin): *drama* (drama), *komma* (comma); (cp. § 34 b)
-*al: kvartal* (3 months), *arsenal* (arsenal)
-*ek: bibliotek* (library), *kartotek* (file)
-*em: system* (system), *problem* (problem)
-*ent: talent* (talent), *instrument* (instrument)
-*et: fakultet* (faculty), *universitet* (university)
-*gram: stenogram* (stenogram), *telegram* (telegram)
-*iv: initiativ* (initiative), *motiv* (motive)
-*ment: departement* (department), *parlament* (parliament)
-*meter: termometer* (thermometer), *barometer* (barometer)*
-*om: fantom* (phantom), *idiom* (idiom)
-*on: leksikon* (encyclopedia, dictionary), *stadion* (stadium)
-*ti: demokrati* (democracy), *aristokrati* (aristocracy)
-*um: gymnasium* (grammar school, high school), *stadium* (phase).

COMPOUNDS *(Sammensetninger)*

§ 36. Norwegian has many more compound nouns than English. Even the use of the hyphen is rather limited, and mainly applied to facilitate the reading of the word. Examples of compounds are *avisartikkel* (newspaper article), *jernbanestasjon* (railway station), *epletre* (apple tree), *bokhylle* (book shelf), *radioapparat* (radio set). In some nouns a genitive -*s*- combines the first and the second element: *uavhengighetserklæring* (declaration of independence), *grunnlovsdag* (constitution day), *universitetslærer* (university teacher). Compounds where the first element is an adjective are: *lavland* (lowland),

---

*) But *meter* (metre, unity of length) and all compounds *(kilometer, centimeter* etc.) are *en*-nouns. Cf. § 20.

bredside (broadside), *allmennutdannelse* (general education); the first element is a verb in *spisestue* (dining room), *kjøpekraft* (buying power).

§ 37. If a compound consists of two or more nouns of different gender, it takes the gender of the last component:
en skole (a school) + *et teater* (a theatre) = *et skoleteater* (a theatre for the schools)
et teater + *en skole* = *en teaterskole* (a theatre school).

THE USE OF THE ARTICLES

§ 38. The **indefinite article** is used mainly as in English, but is omitted in some instances where it is required in English:

a) With predicative nouns denoting a person's **trade, profession, nationality, rank, religion, age,** where they are not preceded by adjectives:

Min far er kjøpmann (My father is **a** business man)
Henrik Wergeland var dikter (Henrik Wergeland was **a** poet)
Joseph Conrad var opprinnelig polakk (Joseph Conrad was originally **a** Pole)
Hans bror er løytnant i flyvåpenet (His brother is **a** lieutenant in the Air Force)
Sigrid Undset ble katolikk (Sigrid Undset became **a** Catholic)
Som gutt ble han sendt til sjøs (As **a** boy he was sent to sea).

b) If the noun is used to characterize the subject in some way or other, the indefinite article is used:

*Han er **en** bedrager*	(He is a deceiver)
*Han er **en** kristen*	(He is a Christian)
*Han er **en** hykler*	(He is a hypocrite)

c) If an individualizing adjective is added, the indefinite article must be applied:
*Min far er en **dyktig** kjøpmann* (My father is an efficient business man)
*Henrik Wergeland var en **stor** dikter* (H. W. was a great poet)
*Han var en **tapper** løytnant i flyvåpenet* (He was a brave lieutenant in the Air Force)
*Sigrid Undset ble en **ivrig** katolikk* (S. U. became an ardent Catholic)

24

d) The indefinite article is not used if the adjective is just classifying:
Han er katolsk biskop (He is a Catholic bishop)
Han er naturalisert engelskmann (He is a naturalized Englishman)

§ 39. The **definite article** occurs in some instances where it is not found in English.

a) In abstract nouns when used in a general sense:
Ungdommen er en herlig tid (Youth is a wonderful time)
Kunsten er lang, men livet er kort (Art is long, but life is short)

b) In connection with names of seasons:
Våren er vakker i Norge (Spring is beautiful in Norway)

c) Nouns denoting measure of time and quantity in a distributive sense:
Han bor her to uker i (or *om*) *året* (He lives here two weeks a year)
Han tjener 15 kroner timen (He earns 15 kroner per hour)
Disse strømpene koster 12 kroner paret (These stockings cost 12 kroner a pair).

§ 40. The definite form is **not** used after genitives: *vårt lands regjering* (our country's government, the government of our country). But the definite form is required when a possessive pronoun is placed after the noun: *sønnen hans* (his son), *landet vårt* (our country). Cf. § 99.

The Adjective *(Adjektivet)*

§ 41. The adjective has an indefinite and a definite form.

The indefinite form *(ubestemt form)* **is applied a) when it stands alone before the noun, b) when it is preceded by an indefinite article, indefinite pronoun or interrogative pronoun, c) when it is used predicatively in a sentence. It agrees in gender and number with the noun or pronoun to which it belongs, adding as a rule -*t* in the neuter, and getting the ending -*e* in the plural, irrespective of gender.**

Examples:
stor by (big city), *en stor by* (a big city), *ingen stor by* (no big city), *hvilken stor by?* (what big city?), *byen er stor* (the city is big).
stor ku (big cow), *ei stor ku* (a big cow), *ingen stor ku* (no big cow), *hvilken stor ku?* (what big cow?), *kua er stor* (the cow is big).

25

stort hus (big house), *et stort hus* (a big house), *intet stort hus* (no big house), *hvilket stort hus?* (what big house?), *huset er stort* (the house is big).

store byer, kuer, hus (big cities, cows, houses), *ingen store byer, kuer, hus* (no big cities, cows, houses), *hvilke store byer, kuer, hus?* (what big cities, cows, houses?), *byene, kuene, husene er store* (the cities, cows, houses are big).

§ 42. a) A final double consonant is reduced to a single one when the neuter *-t* is added:

grønn *kjole* (green dress)   **grønt** *lys* (green light)

b) Exceptions are *full, fullt* (full), *viss, visst* (certain), in order to avoid confusion with the neuters *fult* of *ful* (sly) and *vist* of *vis* (wise).

§ 43. Adjectives ending in a stressed vowel, get *-tt* in the neuter:

ny *bil* (new car)   **nytt** *hus* (new house)

§ 44. Many adjectives do not take *-t* in the neuter:

a) Those already ending in *-t* with a consonant or an unstressed vowel before it:

en **svart** *katt* (a black cat)	*et* **svart** *tøy* (a black material)
en **lett** *sak* (an easy matter)	*et* **lett** *arbeid* (an easy work)
en **fillet** *jakke* (a ragged jacket)	*et* **fillet** *skjørt* (a ragged skirt)*

This rule also applies to past participles (cf. § 120) and to superlatives (cf. § 72):

en **elsket** *lærer* (a beloved teacher)	*et* **elsket** *barn* (a beloved child)
en **solgt** *bil* (a sold car)	*et* **solgt** *hus* (a sold house)
en **stjålet** *sykkel* (a stolen cycle)	*et* **stjålet** *ur* (a stolen watch)
han er **best** (he is best)	*det er* **best** (it is best)

b) Adjectives of more than one syllable ending in *-sk* and all adjectives of *-sk* denoting nationality:**
en **historisk** *begivenhet* (an historical event) – *et* **historisk** *slag* (an historical battle)

*) This ending *-et* meaning "full of" (e.g. *fillet*, full of rags) can also be *-ete* (e.g. *fillete*) in all forms; cf. § 44 f.

) Note that adjectives denoting nationality are **not capitalized in Norwegian; cf. § 18, note.

26

*en **engelsk** avis* (an English paper) – *et **engelsk** skip* (an English ship) – *en **norsk** konsul* (a Norwegian consul) – *et **norsk** frimerke* (a Norwegian stamp)

Other adjectives ending in *-sk* add regularly *t* in the neuter: ***fersk** fisk* (fresh fish) – *ferskt kjøtt* (fresh meat)

c) All adjectives with the suffix *-ig (-lig)*:
*en **fattig** mann* (a poor man) – *et **fattig** land* (a poor country)
*en **vennlig** dame* (a friendly woman) – *et **vennlig** svar* (a friendly answer)

d) Some adjectives ending in a *-d*, of which the most common are *glad* (glad, fond), *redd* (afraid, scared), *lærd* (learned), *fremmed* (foreign), and a large group of foreign words, such as *solid* (solid), *absurd* (absurd), *splendid* (splendid), *perfid* (perfidious), *nitid* (neat). Here belong two adjectives ending in *-t* with vowel before it: *lat* (lazy) and *kåt* (wanton).

e) A few adjectives ending in *-s: gjengs* (current, prevalent), *avleggs* (antiquated, obsolete), *dagligdags* (daily, commonplace), *gammeldags* (oldfashioned), *tilfreds* (contented), *felles* (common, mutual), *sams* (common), *middels* (middling), *stakkars* (poor), *innvortes* (inward), *nymotens* (new-fashioned), *hodekulls* (headlong).

f) Adjectives ending in an unstressed *-e*, for instance: *stille* (calm), *moderne* (modern), *fillete* (ragged; see p. 26 footnote*), *støvete* (dusty); present participles (cf. § 119): *syngende* (singing); comparatives (see §§ 61 and 71): *rikere* (richer), *bedre* (better).

g) Some adjectives ending in *-a*, *-o*, *-u* and *-y*, most of them monosyllabics: *bra* (good), *tro* (faithful), *slu* (cunning), *edru* (sober), *sky* (shy).

h) The synonymous adjectives *likefrem, endefram, liketil* (straightforward).

i) **The neuters of *liten* (small) and *egen* (own) are *lite* and *eget*.**

j) The adjective *megen* (much) is now obsolete and is replaced by the neuter form *mye* (or *meget*), which is also placed in front of nouns of common gender and plural, thus expressing a large quantity of or much of something. Examples: *Jeg har sett mye fattigdom her* (I have seen much poverty here), *vi dyrker mye poteter her i landet* (we grow a lot of potatoes in this country).

SOME IRREGULARITIES ABOUT THE PLURAL
OF ADJECTIVES

§ 45. The ending of the adjective in the plural is *-e: store, trygge, solgte, nye, engelske, fattige, glade, fremmede, gammeldagse, solide*, etc. Cf. § 41.

§ 46. A long *m*-sound in the end of the adjective is doubled in the plural (cf. § 6 *m*):

dum (stupid) – *dumme, tom* (empty) – *tomme, morsom* (amusing) – *morsomme*.

§ 47. a) Adjectives ending in unaccented *-el, -en, -er*, drop the *-e-* before the plural *-e* and a previous double consonant is reduced to a single one:

> *travel* (busy) – *travle*
> *gammel* (old) – *gamle*
>
> *sulten* (hungry) – *sultne*
> *gretten* (peevish) – *gretne*
>
> *mager* (lean) – *magre*
> *vakker* (beautiful) – *vakre*

b) Past participles of strong verbs (cp. §§ 120 and 122) when used attributively change the ending *-et* into *-ne* in the plural: **stjålne** *saker* (stolen things), **håndskrevne** *bøker* (handwritten books).

NB! **funne** *saker* (found things), **forsvunne** *verdener* (lost worlds).

§ 48. In the past participles of weak verbs the ending *-et* (cp. § 126) becomes *-ede* when used attributively: *en* **bortkastet** *dag* (a wasted day), *mange* **bortkastede** *dager* (many wasted days).

§ 49. Some adjectives ending in a vowel get no *-e* in the plural:

blå *biler* (blue cars), **grå** *hester* (grey horses).
This is always the case with the comparatives (see § 71) and present participles (see § 119):
bedre *tider* (better times), **brennende** *spørsmål* (burning questions), and all other adjectives ending in an unaccented *-e:*
stille *stunder* (calm hours), **moderne** *veier* (modern roads).

§ 50. The adjectives mentioned above in § 44 get usually no ending in the plural:

bra *mennesker* (good people).

28

§ 51. **The plural of *liten* (little, small) is *små*:**

*en **liten** bil* (a small car) – *to **små** biler* (two small cars).

DEFINITE FORM *(Bestemt form)*

§ 52. **The definite form of the adjective is identical with the plural in form.
An exception is *liten* (little, small), which is *lille* or *vesle* in the definite
form.**
The definite form is used:

§ 53. after the definite article *den* (common gender), *det* (neuter), *de*
(plural), used with an adjective, all of them rendering English "the":

*den **gode** jord* (the good earth), *det **norske** flagg* (the Norwegian flag),
*de **gamle** menn* (the old men).
In such combinations it is very usual that also the noun, especially
when it is a concrete, has the definite form: *den gode jorden, det
norske flagget, de gamle mennene.*

§ 54. after demonstrative pronouns (cf. § 103) *denne* (common), *dette*
(neuter), *disse* (plural):

*denne **lille** novelle* (this little short-story), *dette **absurde** forslag* (this
absurd proposal), *disse **vakre** barn* (these lovely children).
In such combinations it is usual that also the noun, especially when
it is a concrete, has the definite form: *disse vakre barna* (cf. § 103 b
and c).

§ 55. after personal pronouns (cf. § 85):

*jeg **arme** mann* (I miserable man), *du **heldige** menneske* (you lucky
man).

§ 56. after possessive pronouns (cf. § 100):

*min **gamle** far* (my old father), *din **nye** hatt* (your new hat), *vårt
deilige land* (our beautiful country), *hennes **siste** ord* (her last word).

NB! *egen* in the meaning *own* is used in the indefinite form after
possessive pronouns and genitives (cf. § 57 a):

*min **egen** datter* (my own daughter), *ditt **eget** barn* (your own child),
*Guds **egen** sønn* (God's own son).

§ 57. a) after *s*-genitives of nouns:

*Ibsens **store** drama "Brand"* (Ibsen's great drama "Brand"), *Norges
lange kyst* (Norway's long coast).

b) But not after genitives denoting measures of time and place:
*en times **hardt** arbeid* (one hour's hard work), *en mils **uavbrutt** gange* (one mile's uninterrupted walk).

§ 58. when the adjective constitutes part of the succeeding proper name:
Lille *Eyolf* (Little Eyolf), **Gamle** *Norge* (Old Norway), **Rike Per** *Kremmer* (Rich Peter the Pedlar).

In historical names sometimes placed after the noun:

*Halvdan **Svarte*** (Halfdan the Black), *Harald **Hårfagre*** (Harold the Fairhaired); but **Hellig** *Olav* (Saint Olaf).

§ 59. in exclamations and addresses:

*st**ore** Gud* (great Lord), **kjære** *venn* (dear friend), **elskede** (darling), **lykkelige** *mann* (lucky man).

§ 60. in some expressions where the definite article of the adjective is omitted, especially after a preposition:

hele *dagen* (all day), **halve** *året* (half the year), *i **rette** tid* (at the right moment), *på **rette** måte* (in the right way), *på **høye** tid* (high time), *i **siste** liten* (at the eleventh hour), *midt i **travle** kontortiden* (in the busy office hours), *midt på **lyse** dagen* (in broad daylight), **neste** *gang* (the next time), **neste** *tirsdag**** (Tuesday next week), *for **første** gang* (for the first time), **siste** *dagen* (the last day).

COMPARISON *(Komparasjon)*

§ 61. **The adjectives are compared by adding the endings *-ere* in the comparative and *-est* in the superlative. Adjectives ending in an unstressed *-e* add respectively *-re* and *-st*:**

rik (rich)	*rik**ere*** (richer)	*rik**est*** (richest)
stille (calm)	*stille**re*** (calmer)	*stille**st*** (calmest)

§ 62. Adjectives ending in *-ig* get only *-st* in the superlative. The same is the case with those ending in *-som*, which double the *-m* in the comparative (§ 6 *m*):

billig (cheap)	*billig**ere*** (cheaper)	*billig**st*** (cheapest)
langsom (slow)	*langso**mm**ere* (slower)	*langso**mst*** (slowest)

---

*) Note that the names of days of the week (and the names of the months) are **not** capitalized in Norwegian.

30

§ 63. Adjectives ending in -el, -en, -er, drop the -e- in both comparative and superlative, and a previous double consonant is reduced to a single one:

travel (busy)	*travlere* (busier)	*travlest* (busiest)
ekkel (loathsome)	*eklere* (more loathsome)	*eklest* (most loathsome)
overlegen (haughty)	*overlegnere* (haughtier)	*overlegnest* (haughtiest)
gretten (peevish)	*gretnere* (more peevish)	*gretnest* (most peevish)
mager (lean)	*magrere* (leaner)	*magrest* (leanest)
vakker (beautiful)	*vakrere* (more beautiful)	*vakrest* (most beautiful)

§ 64. The following adjectives form the comparative and superlative by adding respectively -re and -st and changing the stem vowels *a, o, u*:

lang (long)	*lengre* (longer)	*lengst* (longest)
stor (big, great)	*større* (bigger, greater)	*størst* (biggest, greatest)
ung (young)	*yngre* (younger)	*yngst* (youngest)
tung (heavy)	*tyngre* (heavier)	*tyngst* (heaviest)

§ 65. Note the following two adjectives:

få (few)	*færre* (fewer)	*færrest* (fewest)
nær (near)	*nærmere* (nearer)	*nærmest* (nearest)

Example: *i (den) **nærmeste** fremtid* (in the immediate future).

§ 66. The following adjectives form their comparatives and superlatives of a different stem from the positive:

gammel (old)	*eldre* (older, elder)	*eldst* (oldest, eldest)
god (good)	*bedre* (better)	*best* (best)
ille (bad)		
ond (bad, evil)	*verre* (worse)	*verst* (worst)
vond (bad, painful)		
liten (little, small)	*mindre* (less, smaller)	*minst* (least, smallest)
meget (very)	*mer* (more)	*mest* (most)
mye (much)		
mange (many)	*flere* (more)	*flest* (most)

§ 67. The following adjectives appear only in the comparative and the superlative, but corresponding adverbs exist:

bak (behind)	*bakre* (hind, rear)	*bakerst* (hindmost)
bort (away)	*bortre* (farther)	*bortest* (farthest)

fram (forward)	*fremre* (front, anterior)	*fremst* (foremost)
inne (within)	*indre* (inner)	*innerst* (inmost, innermost)
midt (middle)	*midtre*(middle,central)	*midterst* (midmost)
nede (down)	*nedre* (lower)	*nederst* (lowest)
under (under)	*undre* (lower)	*underst* (lowest)
over (over)	*øvre* (upper)	*øverst* (uppermost)
ute (without)	*ytre* (outer)	*ytterst* (outermost, utmost)

§ 68. The following adjectives occur only in the comparative: *høyre* (right), *venstre* (left), *nordre* (northern), *søndre* (southern), *østre* (eastern), *vestre* (western); to the last four adjectives there are the following synonyms: *nordlig, sørlig* or *sydlig, østlig, vestlig.*

§ 69. The following adjectives are only in the superlative: *først* (first), *forrest* (foremost), *sist* (last, latest), *ypperst* (supreme), *mellomst* (middle), *akterst* (aftermost), *eneste* (sole, single).

§ 70. **Norwegian, like English, often compares adjectives by means of *mer* (more) and *mest* (most) whenever the terminations would make the words too long and unwieldy. This is especially the case with polysyllabic adjectives ending in *-sk, -en, -et(e)* (§ 44 and note) and present participle and past participle:**

hysterisk (hysterical)	*mer hysterisk*	*mest hysterisk*
drukken (drunk)	*mer drukken*	*mest drukken*
bakket(e) (hilly)	*mer bakket(e)*	*mest bakket(e)*
strålende (brilliant)	*mer strålende*	*mest strålende*
elsket (beloved)	*mer elsket*	*mest elsket*

§ 71. The comparative is invariable (see § 44 f):

*en **dyrere** bil*	(a more expensive car)
*et **dyrere** hus*	(a more expensive house)
*mange **dyrere** biler, hus*	(many more expensive cars, houses)

§ 72. The superlative form is independant of gender and of number when used predicatively (cf. § 44 a), but takes the ending *-e* in the definite form singular and plural:

*denne bilen er **dyrest***	(this car is most expensive)
*dette huset er **dyrest***	(this house is most expensive)
*disse bilene, husene er **dyrest***	(these cars, houses are most expensive)

den **dyreste** bilen	(the most expensive car)
det **dyreste** huset	(the most expensive house)
de **dyreste** bilene, husene	(the most expensive cars, houses)

THE USE OF COMPARATIVE AND SUPERLATIVE

§ 73. The comparative is often used to denote quite a high degree (absolute comparative):

han er en **eldre** herre nå (he is an elderly gentleman now), vi fikk en **større** ordre fra dette firma i går (we received a substantial order from this firm yesterday), det var et **lettere** sjokk for oss alle (it was quite a bit of a shock to all of us), nå har han bodd i Norge i **lengre** tid (now he has lived in Norway for a length of time), jeg tar gjerne en sigar etter en **bedre** middag (I usually take a cigar after a good dinner), hun er gift med en **høyere** offiser i marinen (she is married to an officer of high rank in the Navy), det er **flere** som tror han har tatt pengene (there are several who believe he has taken the money).

§ 74. The comparative to denote the highest degree in comparison between two does not occur in Norwegian; the superlative is always used: han har to sønner; den **eldste** er ingeniør, den **yngste** skal bli tannlege (he has two sons; the elder is an engineer, the younger is going to be a dentist).

§ 75. Before the positive the strengthening adverb meget (very) can be placed: **meget** god (very good), **meget** stor (very big), **meget** populær (very popular). Before the comparative the strengthening adverb mye (much) is used: **mye** bedre, større, mer populær (much better, bigger, more popular). Cf. § 144.

§ 76. The superlative may be emphasized by aller in front of it: **aller** best (best of all, very best), **aller** størst (very biggest), den **aller** mest populære avis i Norge (the most popular newspaper by far in Norway).

§ 77. Before the superlative the modifying adverb nest (second) may be used: **nest** størst (second biggest), **nest** best (second best), den **nest** siste siden i boken (the last but one page of the book).

ADJECTIVES USED AS NOUNS

§ 78. Adjectives can be used as nouns:

a) in the **common gender singular** without an article, with an indefinite article, a definite article and with a pronoun, and in the **plural** without an article, with a definite article and with a pronoun:

33

*han var avholdt av enhver, både **fattig** og **rik*** (he was loved by everybody, both poor and rich); *legen ble tilkalt til **en syk*** (the doctor was summoned to a sick person); ***den gamle** var verst* (the old one was worst); ***min kjæreste** bor i Bergen* (my dearest one, my sweetheart, lives in Bergen); ***unge** og **gamle** var til stede* (young and old persons were present); *jeg har kjøpt noen gaver til **de små*** (I have bought some presents for the small children); *alle **hans** pårørende var til stede i begravelsen* (all his relatives were present at the funeral).

b) in the **neuter** without an article, with an article, and with a pronoun: *han vet ikke forskjell på **godt** og **ondt*** (he does not know the difference between, he cannot distinguish between, what is good and bad); *man skal prøve alt og velge **det beste*** (one should try everything and choose what is best); *jeg skal gjøre **mitt beste*** (I shall do my best); ***alt godt** kommer fra Gud* (all that is good comes from our Lord).

c) Such adjectives, especially in the definite form, can also appear in the **genitive** case: *han er **de fattiges** formynder* (he is the guardian of the poor); *han hvisket **den elskedes** navn* (he whispered the name of the beloved one); ***de kristnes** Gud* (the God of the Christians); ***det godes** seier i livet* (the victory of what is good in life).

Numerals *(Tallord)*

§ 79. CARDINAL NUMBERS *(Grunntall)*

0 *null*
1 *en* or *én*, neuter *ett*
2 *to*
3 *tre*
4 *fire*
5 *fem*
6 *seks*
7 *sju* (usual form *syv*)
8 *åtte*
9 *ni*
10 *ti*
11 *elleve* (pronounced *elve*)

12 *tolv* (pronounced *tåll;* cf. § 6 *v*)
13 *tretten*
14 *fjorten*
15 *femten*
16 *seksten* (pronounced *seisten;* cf. § 5 and § 6 *k*)
17 *sytten* (usually pronounced *søtten;* cf. § 4 *y*)
18 *atten*
19 *nitten*
20 *tjue* (usual form *tyve*)
21 *tjueen* (usual forms are *en og tjue* or *en og tyve*)
22 *tjueto* (usual forms are *to og tjue* or *to og tyve*)
30 *tretti* (usual form *tredve*)
31 *trettien* (usual forms are *en og tretti* or *en og tredve*)
40 *førti* and *førr*
42 *førtito* (usual forms are *to og førti* or *to og førr*)
50 *femti*
54 *femtifire* (usual form *fire og femti*)
60 *seksti*
67 *sekstisju* (usual forms are *sju og seksti* or *syv og seksti*)
70 *sytti* (usual pronunciation *søtti;* cf. § 4 *y*)
80 *åtti*
90 *nitti*
100 *hundre* or *ett hundre*
110 *hundre og ti* or *ett hundre og ti*
200 *to hundre*
700 *sju hundre* (usual form *syv hundre*)
1 000 *tusen* or *ett tusen*
2 000 *to tusen*
10 000 *ti tusen*
15 000 *femten tusen*
40 000 *førti tusen*
52 614 *femtito tusen seks hundre og fjorten* (usual form *to og femti tusen* etc.)
100 000 *hundre tusen* or *ett hundre tusen*
500 000 *femhundre tusen* or *en halv million*
1 000 000 *en million*
3 500 000 *tre millioner fem hundre tusen* or *tre og en halv million*
100 000 000 *hundre millioner* or *ett hundre millioner*
1 000 000 000 *en milliard*
2 000 000 000 *to milliarder*
1 000 000 000 000 *en million millioner* or *en billion**

¹) Note that *en billion* is not the American **one billion,** but **one trillion.**

An official change was made in the numerals through the spelling reform of 1938, introducing *sju* (formerly *syv*), *tjue* (formerly *tyve*) etc. In 1951 the English way of saying the tens before the digits was adopted: *femtifire* (formerly *fire og femti*). Since, however, the old forms are still in frequent use, they have been added in parenthesis.

The Use of Cardinal Numbers

§ 80. The figures from 1 to 9 are called respectively *et ett-tall, totall, tretall, firetall* etc. When the figures are used for grading purposes, they are called *en ener, en toer, en treer, en firer, en femmer* etc. In colloquial language *en femmer, en tier* means a "five-", resp. "ten-kroner note". As will be seen from the above list, all cardinal numbers from 13 to 19 end in *-ten*. Thence the expression *en tenåring*, which renders "a teenager".

The numbers *hundre, tusen, million, milliard, billion* are really nouns; *hundre* and *tusen*, however, get no ending in the plural except when they are used to express *hundrer av, tusener av* (hundreds of, thousands of).

Some Expressions with Cardinal Numbers

§ 81. $3 + 8 = 11$ *tre og* (or *pluss*) *åtte er elleve*

$16 - 9 = 7$ *seksten minus ni er sju*, or *ni fra seksten er sju*

$10 \times 9 = 90$ *ti ganger ni er nitti*

$18 : 6 = 3$ *atten dividert med seks er tre*, or *atten delt på seks er tre*, or *seks i atten går en tregang*

Pakken koster kr. 2,50, *to kroner og femti (øre)*, or *to femti*, or *to og en halv krone*, or *to og en halv* (the packet costs kroner 2,50); *klokken er åtte* (it is eight o'clock), *klokken er fem (minutter) over åtte* (it is five [minutes] past eight), *den er femten minutter over*, or *et kvarter over* or *kvart over, åtte* (it is fifteen minutes [a quarter] past eight), *den er ti (minutter) på halv ni* (it is 20 minutes past eight), *den er halv ni* (it is half past eight), *den er ti (minutter) over halv ni* (it is twenty minutes to nine), *den er femten minuter på*, or *et kvarter på* or *kvart på, ni* (it is a quarter to nine), *den er fem (minutter) på ni* (it is five minutes to nine); *han debuterte tidlig på syttitallet* (he had his debut early in the seventies), *hans innflytelse var størst i femtiårene* (his influence was greatest in the fifties).

Henrik Wergeland ble født i atten hundre og åtte or *atten åtte* (Henrik Wergeland was born in 1808), *jeg er født i nitten hundre og femten* or *nitten femten* (I was born in 1915). Note that the present tense is used about living individuals, the past tense about deceased persons. Cf. § 134 b.

Note the following collective numbers: *et par dager senere* (a couple of days later), *et par-tre uker* (two or three weeks), *et par sko* (a pair of shoes), *et dusin* (a dozen), *en tylft* (twelve, used about timber, pit-props etc.), *et snes* (a score), *et gross* (a gross).

The form with *hundre* can only be used about figures up to and including *nitten hundre*. Above that must be used *to tusen* (2000), *tre tusen* (3000), *tre tusen fem hundre* (3500) etc.

ORDINAL NUMBERS *(Ordenstall)*

§ 82.
1. *(den* or *det) første*
2. —,,— *annen* (pronounced *aen*) or *andre*
3. —,,— *tredje*
4. —,,— *fjerde* (pronounced *fjære;* cf. § 4 *e* and § 6 *d*)
5. —,,— *femte*
6. —,,— *sjette*
7. —,,— *sjuende* (usual form *syvende*)
8. —,,— *åttende*
9. —,,— *niende*
10. —,,— *tiende*
11. —,,— *ellevte*
12. —,,— *tolvte* (pronounced *tållte*)
13. —,,— *trettende*
14. —,,— *fjortende*
15. —,,— *femtende*
16. —,,— *sekstende* (pronounced *seistene;* cf. § 5 and § 6 *k*)
17. —,,— *syttende* (usually pronounced *søttene;* cf. § 4 *y*)
18. —,,— *attende*
19. —,,— *nittende*
20. —,,— *tjuende* (usual form *tyvende*)
21. —,,— *tjueførste* (usual forms are *en og tjuende* or *en og tyvende*)
22. —,,— *tjueandre* (usual forms are *to og tjuende* or *to og tyvende*)
30. —,,— *trettiende* (usual form *tredevte*)
31. —,,— *trettiførste* (usual form *en og tredevte*)
40. —,,— *førtiende*
42. —,,— *førtiandre* (usual form is *to og førtiende*)
50. —,,— *femtiende*
54. —,,— *femtifjerde* (usual form *fire og femtiende*)
60. —,,— *sekstiende*
67. —,,— *sekstisjuende* (usual forms are *sju og sekstiende* or *syv og sekstiende*)

70. *(den* or *det) syttiende* (usual pronunciation *søttiende;* cf. § 4 *y*)
80. —,,— *åttiende*
90. —,,— *nittiende*
100. —,,— *hundrede*
110. —,,— *hundre og tiende*
200. —,,— *to hundrede*
1000. —,,— *tusende*
2000. —,,— *to tusende*

With regard to the changes brought about by recent spelling reforms, see § 79.

§ 83. The forms *annen, annet* are mostly used to render "second", whereas *den andre, det andre* will stand for "the other" (see § 109 g). *Dronning Elizabeth* **den annen** (Queen Elizabeth the Second), *han går i* **annen** *klasse* (he goes to the second form [grade]), *vi begynner med* **annet** *avsnitt* (we begin with the second paragraph), *den første verdenskrigen begynte i 1914,* **den annen** *verdenskrig begynte i 1939* (the first world war began in 1914, the second world war began in 1939); *den andre* or *det andre* has its counterpart in *den ene* or *det ene,* the only cardinal number that can be inflected in gender: *han gav meg to roser;* **den ene** *var gul,* **den andre** *var rød* (he gave me two roses; the one was yellow, the other was red), *jeg har to barn;* **det ene** *er en gutt,* **det andre** *er en pike* (I have two children; the one is a boy, the other is a girl).

Bjørnson ble født (den) åttende desember 1832 (Björnson was born on the 8th December 1832), *Norge fikk sin grunnlov (den) syttende mai 1814* (Norway got her constitution on the 17th May 1814). **NB!** Norwegian has no preposition equivalent to "on" before dates or "of" before the name of the month. The number in dates cannot be placed after the name of the month, like English "May 17", etc.

Vi lever i (det) tjuende århundre or *hundreår* (we are living in the 20th century). This could also be said: *Vi lever på nittenhundretallet.*

FRACTIONS *(Brøker)*

§ 84. a) In fractions the numerator is a cardinal number, and so is the denominator, but with the addition of the ending *-del,* plural *-deler: en femtendel* ($^1/_{15}$), *to femtendeler* ($^2/_{15}$), *en tjuefemdel* ($^1/_{25}$), *to tjuefemdeler* ($^2/_{25}$), *en hundredel* ($^1/_{100}$), *to hundredeler* ($^2/_{100}$).

b) The traditional way of making fractions was to use ordinal numbers in the denominator. This was officially changed in 1951 but is still the method most frequently heard: e. g. *en femtendedel, to femtendedeler, en fem og tjuendedel* or *en fem og tyvendedel, to fem og tjuendedeler* or *to fem og tyvendedeler, en hundrededel, to hundrededeler.* This way of making fractions is optional in the case of numbers up to 12: *en tredel* or *en tredjedel* ($1/_3$), *to tredeler* or *to tredjedeler* ($2/_3$), *en åttedel* or *en åttendedel* ($1/_8$), *fem seksdeler* or *fem sjettedeler* ($5/_6$), *en tolvdel* or *en tolvtedel* ($1/_{12}$).

c) Instead of *en firedel* or *en fjerdedel* ($1/_4$) is often said *en kvart* and before a neuter noun *et kvart:* e. g. *en kvart flaske* ($1/_4$ bottle), *et kvart glass* (one quarter of a glass). The fraction $1/_2$ is always pronounced *en halv*, which is declined like an adjective in gender and number: e. g. *en halv flaske* (half a bottle), *et halvt glass* (half a glass), *to halve flasker, glass* (two half bottles, glasses).

d) In compound fractions where the numerator is 1, a succeeding noun is in the singular:
fire og en halv flaske (four and a half bottles), *tre og en halv krone* (three and a half kroner).

e) The number $1^1/_2$ is either read *en og en halv* (neuter *et og et halvt*) or *halvannen* (neuter *halvannet*) with the following noun in the singular: *en og en halv krone* or *halvannen krone* (one and a half kroner), *et og et halvt år* or *halvannet år* (one and a half years).

Pronouns *(Pronomener)*

PERSONAL PRONOUNS *(Personlige pronomener)*

§ 85. a) **Singular.**

	1st person	2nd person	3rd person
Subj.	*jeg* (I)	*du, De* (you)	*han* (he), *hun* (she), *den, det* (it)
Obj.	*meg* (me)	*deg, Dem* (you)	*ham* (him), *henne* (her), *den, det* (it)

b) **Plural.**

	1st person	2nd person	3rd person
Subj.	*vi* (we)	*dere* (you)	*de* (they)
Obj.	*oss* (us)	*dere* (you)	*dem* (them)

§ 86. The object form is used as object, indirect object and when governed by prepositions.

§ 87.   a) **Note:** *du* and *deg* (just like the possessive pronouns *din, ditt, dine;* see § 98 a) **can be used only in familiar conversation among persons who are intimate friends, when we are speaking to children, relatives, schoolmates, who are, as we say,** *"dus"*.

Examples:
Du er min beste venn (You are my best friend)
Vil du ta med deg mitt brev, mor? (Will you take with you my letter, mother?)

b) **People with whom we are not well acquainted, must always be addressed** *De, Dem* (like the possessive pronoun *Deres;* cp. § 98 a and b).

Examples:
Vil De ha en kopp kaffe? (Will you have a cup of coffee?)
Jeg så Dem i teatret i går (I saw you in the theatre yesterday)

§ 88.   a) Predicatively the object forms are normally used: *Det er meg* (It is I), *er det Dem?* (is it you?). But the subject form can also be used, especially when followed by a relative clause where the relative pronoun is subject: *det var han som gjorde det* (it was he who did it).

b) The object form is also used in comparisons with the subject: *han er eldre enn meg* (he is older than I), *du spiller bedre enn ham* (you play better than he).
But also the subject form can be used: *hun skriver fortere enn du* (she writes faster than you).

§ 89.   The pronouns *den, det* are used about things or objects of respectively common gender and neuter gender: *Båten ble bygd i Glasgow, og vi kjøpte den i fjor* (The ship was built in Glasgow, and we bought it last year). *Huset ble bygd for fem år siden, men vi kjøpte det i fjor* (The house was built five years ago, but we bought it last year).

§ 90.   In the 3rd person singular the pronouns *han, hun* are sometimes used not only of persons or human beings, but also about animals, things and inanimate beings when they are personified: e. g. *reven, han er lur* (the fox, he is sly), *kua er et nyttig dyr; hun gir oss melk* (the cow is a useful animal; she gives us milk); *nå går han godt* (now he, i. e. the car, runs nicely); *i dag er han* (viz. *fjorden) så blank som et speil* (today he, i. e. the fiord, is shining like a mirror); *hun* (viz. *seilbåten) ligger for anker nå* (she, i. e. the sailboat, is lying at anchor now).

§ 91. Sometimes the adverbs *her* (here) and *der* (there) are added to the pronouns in the 3rd person to indicate something near and far away: *han her er min sønn* (this is my son), *han der er en venn av min sønn* (that is a friend of my son), *jeg beholder den her* (I keep this one), *jeg liker best den der* (I like that one best). Cf. § 103 b and c.

§ 92. Instead of the personal pronoun *dere* in the 2nd person plural the *I,* *eder* are sometimes found in elevated, especially biblical style: *I skal* *være mine vitner* (Ye shal be witnesses unto me), *Se, jeg forkynner* ***eder*** *en stor glede* (Behold, I bring you good tidings of great joy). Cp. § 98 c.

§ 93. The object forms of the personal pronouns in the 1st and 2nd persons singular and plural are used as reflexive pronouns corresponding to the English ones ending in "-self", "-selves": *jeg morer **meg*** (I enjoy myself), *du morer **deg*** (you enjoy yourself), *De morer **Dem*** (you enjoy yourself), *vi morer **oss*** (we enjoy ourselves), *dere morer **dere*** (you enjoy yourselves). In the 3rd person singular and plural the *seg* is used. See § 96.

THE USE OF *DET*

§ 94. As seen above the neuter *det* is applied when it refers to a noun of neuter gender. In addition, *det* is used:

a) in impersonal expressions, formal subjects, corresponding to English "it": *det regner* (it is raining), *det snør* (it is snowing), *det blåser* (it is blowing), *det er varmt* (it is hot), *det er dyrt å røyke* (it is expensive to smoke, smoking is expensive), *hva er det?* (what is it, what is the matter?), *hvordan står det til?* (how is it with you, how are you?), *hvordan går det?* (how goes it?)

b) corresponding to the English "there" in expressions like "there are": e.g. *det var engang en konge som hadde en datter* (there once was a king who had a daughter), *det er mange mennesker i teatret i aften* (there are many people in the theatre this evening), *er det en postkasse i nærheten?* (is there a mailbox in the neighbourhood?). This construction is also found in the case of verbs with the same meaning as *være* (be): e. g. *det **fins** fremdeles mange slike hoteller i landet* (there are still many such hotels in the country), *det eksisterer ikke noen lege ved det navn* (there is [exists] no doctor of that name).

§ 95. In many instances the pronoun *det* has no equivalent in English when the real subject is a noun in the indefinite form with an indefinite

41

article, or if it is or contains an indefinite pronoun like *noen* (some, any), *mange* (many), *flere* (several, more), *få* (few), *ingen* (no, nobody):

a) when the predicate is an intransitive verb and especially when an adverbial phrase denoting place is added: *det kom en mann gående nedover gaten* (a man came walking down the street), *det falt en sten fra mitt hjerte* (a stone fell from my heart, i. e. a load was lifted from my mind), *det har bodd mange nordmenn her* (many Norwegians have been living here), *det kommer ingen gjester i aften* (no guests are coming to-night).

b) when the predicate is in the passive (§§ 129–133): *det fødes flere gutter enn piker* (more boys than girls are born), *det ble funnet en vakker diamantring i hagen* (a beautiful diamond ring was found in the garden), *det er ikke tatt noen bestemmelse ennå* (no decision has been made yet), *det ble satt i gang undersøkelser overalt* (inquiries were made everywhere), *det ble drept mange ved bilulykker den dagen* (many people were killed in motor-car accidents that day), *det fortelles så mangt om ham* (so much is told about him), *det ble bygd flere hus i 1950* (several houses were built in 1950).

c) This construction is not applicable when the subject is a definite noun: *husene ble bygd i 1950* (the houses were built in 1950), *den gamle mannen kom gående nedover gaten* (the old man came walking down the street).

The indicating *det* can however be used when the definite form has indefinite meaning: e. g. *det oppstod den største vanskelighet i forbindelse med eksporten* (a very great difficulty arose in connection with the export); but, *den største vanskelighet oppstod i forbindelse med eksporten* (the greatest difficulty, i. e. the greatest of all the difficulties, arose in connection with the export).

d) With the verb *være* (be) the pronoun *det* is often used about persons and things of common gender and plural mentioned immediately before.

In these cases English must use "he", "she", "they". *Hvem er den gutten? Det er min sønn* (Who is that boy? He is my son). *Her ser du to pene piker. Det er Marie og Ellen* (Here you see two pretty girls. They are Marie and Ellen). Cf. § 103 g.

REFLEXIVE PRONOUNS *(Refleksive pronomener)*

§ 96. a) The English reflexive pronouns in the 1st and 2nd persons singular and plural – "myself", "yourself", "ourselves", "yourselves" – are rendered by the respective personal pronouns *meg, deg* and *Dem*,

42

oss, dere (cp. § 93). **The reflexive pronoun in the 3rd person singular and plural is** *seg*, corresponding to English "himself", "herself", "itself", "themselves". All these pronouns refer to the subject of the clause in which they occur.

jeg morer meg – I enjoy myself
du morer deg – you enjoy yourself
De morer Dem – you enjoy yourself (see § 87 a and b)
han, hun, mannen, barnet morer seg – he, she, the man, the child
                            enjoys him-, her-, itself
vi morer oss – we enjoy ourselves
dere morer dere – you enjoy yourselves
de, mennene, barna morer seg – they, the men, the children, enjoy
                            themselves

The same pronouns are used after prepositions, where English too takes the personal pronouns: *jeg har penger på meg* (I have money on me), *du har penger på deg* (you have money on you), *De har penger på Dem* (you have money on you), *han, hun, mannen, barnet har penger på seg* (he, she, the man, the child has money on him, her, it), *vi har penger på oss* (we have money on us), *dere har penger på dere* (you have money on you), *de har penger på seg* (they have money on them).

b) There are many reflexive verbs in Norwegian which are not reflexive in English. They are always listed with *seg* in the infinitive, and can be followed by an object or a preposition: e. g. *barbere seg* (shave), *bry seg om* (care about), *gifte seg med* (marry), *sikre seg* (secure), *påta seg* (undertake), *sette seg* (sit down), *snyte seg* (blow one's nose).

c) The Norwegian *selv* (cf. § 105 a), corresponding to English "self", "selves", is used only when it is emphasized that the action in the verb refers to one's own person, not to others.

Jeg kan more meg selv (I can enjoy myself)
du kan more deg selv (you can enjoy yourself)
De kan more Dem selv (you can enjoy yourself)
han, hun, mannen, barnet kan more seg selv
(he, she, the man, the child, can enjoy himself, herself, itself)
vi kan more oss selv (we can enjoy ourselves)
dere kan more dere selv (you can enjoy yourselves)
de kan more seg selv (they can enjoy themselves)

viz. without being dependent on others

RECIPROCAL PRONOUNS *(Resiproke pronomener)*

§ 97. The reciprocal pronouns are the synonymous *hinannen, hverandre* (one another, each other). They can be used in the genitive case *hinannens, hverandres.*

Examples:

Vi må hjelpe hverandre (we must help each other), *brødrene har aldri sett hinannen* (the brothers have never seen one another), *de bærer hverandres* (or *hinannens*) *byrder* (they carry each other's burdens).

POSSESSIVE PRONOUNS *(Eiendomspronomener)*

§ 98. a) The possessive pronouns denoting ownership of thing or things to which they are attached, are: 1st person singular *min*, 2nd person singular familiar *din*, 2nd person singular formal *Deres* (cp. § 87 b), 3rd person singular *hans* (masculine), *hennes* (feminine), *dens* (common gender), *dets* (neuter gender), 1st person plural *vår*, 2nd and 3rd persons plural *deres*. Only the following pronouns agree in gender and number with the attached noun:

min bil	– *mitt hus*	– *mine biler, hus*
(my car)	(my house)	(my cars, houses)
din sønn	– *ditt barn*	– *dine sønner, barn*
(your son)	(your child)	(your sons, children)
vår far	– *vårt vindu*	– *våre fedre, vinduer*
(our father)	(our window)	(our fathers, windows).

b) The other possessives have the same form regardless of the gender and number of the nouns to which they are attached:

Deres		your
hans	*(bil, sønn, far, hus,*	his (car, son, father, house,
hennes	*barn, land,*	her child, country,
dens	*sønner, fedre, hus, biler,*	its sons, fathers, houses, cars,
dets	*barn, land)*	its children, countries)
deres		your
deres		their

c) Like the personal pronouns *I, eder* (see § 92) the possessive *eders* in the 2nd person plural is sometimes found in elevated, especially biblical, style: **Eders** *hjerter forferdes ikke* (Let not your hearts be troubled).

44

d) **The reflexive possessive pronoun** *sin*, **which varies in gender and number like** *min*, *din* (see above a) renders "his", "her", "hers", "its", "their" "theirs". **Thus it is used only in the 3rd person singular and plural, and like the reflexive personal pronoun** *seg* (see § 96 a) **it refers to the subject of the clause in which it occurs.**

Mannen solgte sitt hus (the man sold his house), *han gikk sin vei* (he went his way), *hun tok sin sønn med seg* (she took her son with her), *barnet mistet sin sykkel* (the child lost its cycle), *guttene gikk til sin skole* (the boys went to their school), *barna besøkte sin far i sine ferier* (the children visited their father in their holidays).

NB! As the reflexive possessive pronouns must always refer to the subject of the sentence, it is a matter of course that they can never be or constitute part of the subject. In those cases the pronouns *hans, hennes, dens, dets, deres* have to be applied.

e) Norwegian has no special equivalent to the English possessive pronouns "mine", "yours", "hers", "ours", "theirs", which are also rendered by *min, din* or *Deres, hennes* or *sin, vår, deres* or *sin*.

Min fars bil er eldre enn din (my father's car is older than yours), *min er eldst* (mine is oldest), *ditt hus er større enn mitt* (your house is bigger than mine), *den lille gutten der er min* (that little boy is mine), *er de barna Deres?* (are those children yours?), *det hvite huset til høyre på bildet er vårt* (the white house on the right side of the picture is ours), *jeg tok min bil og min søster tok sin* (I took my car and my sister took hers), *denne pennen er hennes* (this pen is hers), *disse syklene er ikke deres* (these cycles are not theirs).

f) For the English phrases "a friend of **mine**", "an acquaintance of **yours**" Norwegian has constructions with the personal pronouns: *en venn av **meg**, en kjenning av **deg**.*

g) A peculiar use of the possessive pronoun in the 1st and 2nd person singular is found in exclamations of abusive terms, where the English employ the personal pronoun: *jeg, min idiot!* (I, silly fool!), *ditt fe! din tosk!* (you fool!).

Position of Possessives

§ 99. In all the above examples the possessive pronouns used as adjectives precede the nouns to which they belong. **There is, however, a tendency to place the pronouns after the definite form of the nouns:** e. g. *bilen min* (my car), *huset mitt* (my house), *sønnene hennes* (her sons) instead of *min bil, mitt hus, hennes sønner*. This is mostly the case in colloquial speech and in connections where the noun is concrete. Note the difference in meaning between the following sentences:

kirken vår ble bygd i 1858 (our church, i. e. the building, was erected in 1858), but *vår kirke er bygd på kristendommens grunn* (our Church, i. e. the institution, is built on the foundation of Christianity).

§ 100. An adjective after the possessive pronoun takes the definite form (see § 56):

min (din, hans, hennes, sin, vår, deres) **nye** *bil* – my (your, his, her, our, their) new car

mitt (ditt, hans, hennes, sitt, vårt, deres) **nye** *hus* – my (your, his, her, our, their) new house

mine (dine, hans, hennes, sine, våre, deres) **nye** *biler, hus* – my (your, his, her, our, their) new cars, houses

§ 101. Also in such cases the possessive pronoun may be placed after the definite form of the noun (cf. § 99), but then the noun must be preceded by the definite article *den, det, de* plus the definite form of the adjective:

den nye bilen min (din, hans, hennes, sin, vår, deres)
det nye huset mitt (ditt, hans, hennes, sitt, vårt, deres)
de nye bilene, husene, mine (dine, hans, hennes, sine, våre, deres)

§ 102. In the following cases, where the English language takes the possessive pronoun before parts of the body or apparel, Norwegian has the definite article:

han ristet på hodet (he shook his head), *jeg brente fingrene* (I burnt my fingers), *han satt med hendene i lommene* (he sat with his hands in his pockets).

DEMONSTRATIVE PRONOUNS *(Påpekende pronomener)*

§ 103. a) **The chief demonstrative pronouns are** *den* (that, that one), *denne* (this, this one), *hin* (that, that yonder). They are all inflected in gender and number. When standing alone they can take a genitive case, but only the plural of *den* has a special object form:

	Common	Neuter	Plural
Nom.	*den* (that)	*det* (that)	*de* (those)
Gen.	*dens*	*dets*	*deres*
			obj. *dem*
Nom.	*denne* (this)	*dette* (this)	*disse* (these)
Gen.	*dennes*	*dettes*	*disses*
Nom.	*hin* (that)	*hint* (that)	*hine* (those)
Gen.	*hins*	*hints*	*hines*

b) *Den (det, de)*, which has the same form as, but stronger stress in pronunciation than, the definite article of the adjective (§ 53), is used to indicate somebody or something remote from the speaking person. This function is often emphasized by the placing of the adverb *der* (there) after the pronoun or after the noun attached. Further, it is characteristic of Norwegian that the noun after demonstrative pronouns often appears in the definite form (cf. §§ 53 and 54).

c) *Denne (dette, disse)* is used about persons and objects in the immediate vicinity of the speaker. This is often emphasized by placing the adverb *her* (here) after the pronoun or after the noun attached. The succeeding noun often appears in the definite form (cf. §§ 53 and 54).

d) *Hin (hint, hine)* is rarely used now, and only in literary language. It refers mostly to remote things.

Examples:

denne boken (her) er billigere enn den (der) (this book is cheaper than that), *din bror kjøpte den, så jeg synes du bør ta denne* (your brother bought that, so I think you ought to take this), *vil du gi meg den kniven der* (will you give me that knife), *i de dager bodde jeg i Wales* (in those days I lived in Wales), *vi elsker dette landet* (we love this country), *hvert år kommer mange turister fra det landet* (every year many tourists come from that country), *disse maleriene har jeg kjøpt i Frankrike* (I have bought these paintings in France), *de maskinene får vi fra utlandet* (we get those machines from abroad), *dette og hint* (this and that), *jeg har aldri sett den guttens make* (I have never seen the likes of that boy), *dette landets næringsveier er først og fremst jordbruk og skipsfart* (the livelihoods of this country are first and foremost agriculture and shipping), *dennes far utvandret til Amerika* (this person's father emigrated to America).

e) The indefinite form of the noun after the pronoun is more usual in literary language and in abstracts: *denne filosofi fikk stor innflytelse i Europa* (this philosophy had great influence in Europe), *denne idé er gammel* (this idea is old).

f) The pronoun *den (det, de)* is used when it, or the noun to which it belongs, is the antecedent of a relative clause that cannot be left out. In such cases English has "he", "the man", "that", "those", "the one(s)", or just the definite article in front of the noun: *den som finner uret, vil få en belønning* (he who finds the watch will get a reward), *selv den som har levd det meste av sitt liv i utlandet, elsker sitt land* (even the man who has lived most of his life abroad, loves his country), *jeg vil gi denne ringen til den som kan svømme fortest* (I will give this ring to the one who can swim fastest), *det skuespill som er best kjent, er «Peer Gynt»* (the play that is best known, is "Peer Gynt").

g) **When the demonstrative pronoun** (like the personal pronoun *det*, see § 95 d) **has the function of pointing to things and persons being observed or mentioned immediately before but coming after the verb *være*, the neuters *det* and *dette* are applied also about nouns of common gender and plural:** *dette er min sønn* (this is my son), *det er en dårlig film* (that is a bad film), *dette er mine barn* (these are my children), *det der er gode epler* (those are good apples), *dette var hans siste innvendinger* (these were his last objections), *det var sørgelige dager* (those were sad days). But: *denne sønnen er min* (this son is mine), *den filmen er dårlig* (that film is bad), *disse barna er mine* (these children are mine), *de eplene der er gode* (those apples are good), *disse innvendingene var hans siste* (these objections were his last), *de dager var sørgelige* (those days were sad).

§ 104. Among the demonstratives are also classed the following pronouns; they have no cases other than the nominative.

Common		Neuter	Plural
sådan		*sådant*	*sådanne*
sånn	(such)	*sånt*	*sånne*
slik		*slikt*	*slike*

These three are nearly synonyms, although *sådan* is a bit literary and *sånn* somewhat colloquial. The word *så* (so) has sometimes a demonstrative function: *i så tilfelle* (in such a case), *i så måte* (in that respect), *i så henseende* (in that respect).

§ 105. a) The demonstrative pronoun *selv* ("self", "-self", "-selves") is indeclinable in gender and number and is placed after the noun to which it belongs. However, it can also precede the noun, but has then the form *selve* in all genders and numbers: *kongen selv* (the king himself), *barnet selv* (the child itself), *guttene selv* (the boys themselves) or: *selve kongen, selve barnet, selve guttene*. The form *selv* in front of the noun has the meaning "even": *selv kongen kunne ikke gjøre noe* (even the king could not do anything).

b) *begge* (both) is only applicable in the plural. This pronoun also stands for "either" of two: *vi har epletrær på begge sider* (we have appletrees on either side), *vi kan si begge deler* (we can say either, both).

48

RELATIVE PRONOUNS *(Relative pronomener)*

§ 106. a) **The chief relative pronoun is** *som*, **which stands for** "who", "whom", "which", "that"*, "as". This implies that *som*, which is indeclinable, refers to persons, things, ideas, etc. in both singular and plural, whether the relative clause is defining or non-defining.

Examples: *han har en søster **som** bor i Bergen* (he has a sister **who** lives in Bergen), *Nansen, **som** alle nordmenn kjenner, fikk Nobels fredspris i 1922* (Nansen, **whom** all Norwegians know, was awarded the Nobel peace prize in 1922), *Oslo, **som** er Norges hovedstad, har omtrent en halv million innbyggere* (Oslo, **which** is the capital of Norway, has approximately half a million inhabitants), *den bilen **som** jeg hadde i fjor, har jeg solgt* (I have sold the car **that** I had last year), *vi er slikt stoff **som** drømmer er gjort av* (we are such stuff **as** dreams are made of).

b) As in English, a relative pronoun can be omitted, when not the subject, in defining clauses: *den kniven (som) jeg gav ham, er laget i Sheffield* (the knife [that] I gave him was made in Sheffield), *kjenner du den mannen (som) jeg lånte pengene?* (do you know the man to whom I lent the money?).

c) **Prepositions governing the relative pronoun** *som* **are always placed at the end of the clause:** *der ser du huset som jeg bor i* (there you see the house in which I live), *han er en mann (som) jeg har lært mye av* (he is a man from whom I have learnt much).

d) The genitive of the relative pronoun is *hvis*, corresponding to both "whose" and "of which". It can be used about persons or things, abstracts as well as concretes: *denne mannen, hvis bøker blir lest av både unge og gamle, er Bjørnson* (this man, whose books are read by both young and old, is Björnson), *krigen, hvis utfall lenge var usikkert, varte i over fem år* (the war, the issue of which was long uncertain, lasted for more than five years), *det er en religion hvis tilhengere er spredt over hele verden* (it is a religion whose adherents are spread all over the world).

There is a tendency in Norwegian to avoid the genitive *hvis* and to replace it by other constructions: e. g. *denne mannen er Bjørnson, og hans bøker blir lest av både unge og gamle; krigen varte i over fem år, og dens utfall var lenge usikkert; det er en religion som har tilhengere spredt over hele verden.*

e) Other relative pronouns of a more literary character are *der, hvem, hvilken, hva:*

---

*) **NB!** Do not confuse the relative pronoun "that" *(som)* with the subordinating conjunction "that" *(at)*. Cp. § 111 h.

der is sometimes used as the subject in order to bring about a variation from a previous or succeeding *som:* e. g. *ingen kjente ham, der var reist hjemmefra som liten gutt* (nobody knew him who had left home as a little boy).

hvem (whom), indeclinable, is used about persons and cannot be the subject of a sentence. It occurs only in very literary and formal language: *det er en mann hvem jeg skylder stor takknemlighet* (that is a man to whom I owe great gratitude), *han elsker eskimoene, blant hvem han har tilbrakt nesten femten år av sitt liv* (he loves the eskimoes, with whom he has spent nearly fifteen years of his life).

hvilken (neuter *hvilket*, plural *hvilke*), which is not used as a subject of the sentence, refers to both persons and things. It is also quite literary, but like the previous *hvem* it is applied in order to avoid clumsy use of a preposition at the end of a sentence: *den dalen gjennom hvilken elven flyter, er meget flat* (the valley, through which the river flows, is very flat), *jeg så de lange fjellkjeder, bak hvilke solen nettopp gikk ned* (I saw the long mountain ranges, behind which the sun was just setting).

The neuter form *hvilket* has often reference to the contents of the previous clause, like "which" in English, and can also be the subject: *han hadde studert spansk, hvilket var en stor fordel for ham da han kom til Mexico* (he had studied Spanish, which was a great advantage to him when he came to Mexico).

hva has the same function: *han er en av Norges beste idrettsmenn, hva ingen vil benekte* (he is one of the leading sportsmen of Norway, which nobody will deny).

Instead of applying *hvilket* and *hva* to refer to a previous clause, it is more common to use the construction *noe som* or to make two parallel principal clauses: *han hadde studert spansk, noe som var en stor fordel for ham*, etc. or *han hadde studert spansk, og det var*, etc.; *han er en av Norges beste idrettsmenn, noe som ingen vil benekte*, or *han er en av Norges beste idrettsmenn; det vil ingen benekte*.

hva is quite usual after *alt* (all), thus forming an indefinite relative (see below): *alt hva vi har, vil vi dele med hverandre* (all that we have, we will share with each other).

§ 107. INDEFINITE RELATIVE PRONOUNS
(Ubestemte relative pronomener)

corresponding to the English pronouns ending in "-ever" or "-soever" are: *hvem* or *hvem som* or *hvem som helst som* (whoever) used only of persons: e. g. *jeg hilste på hvem (hvem som, hvem som helst som) jeg møtte* (I greeted whomever I met); *hvem . . . enn* has the same function and meaning: *jeg er uinteressert i hvem du enn ansetter* (I am uninterested in whomever you appoint); *hva,* or *hva som,* or *hva som helst som, hva . . . enn* (whatever) refer to things only: *her kan du få hva* (or *hva som helst) du (enn) vil* (here you can get whatever you like); *hvilken (hvilket, hvilke)* or *hvilken (hvilket, hvilke) som helst som* or *hvilken (hvilket, hvilke) . . . enn* (whoever, whichever) and *enhver* or *enhver (ethvert) som helst som* (whoever, whichever) can refer to both persons and things: *du kan velge hvilken bok du vil ha* (you can select whichever book you want).

INTERROGATIVE PRONOUNS *(Spørrende pronomener)*

§ 108. a) The interrogative pronouns are *hvem* (who, whom, which) referring to persons, and *hva* (what) having reference to things and inanimate objects. Both *hvem* and *hva* have noun function only. A governing preposition is usually placed at the end of the sentence:

Examples:

hvem bor der? (who lives there?), *hvem skal du møte på stasjonen?* (whom are you going to meet at the station?), *hvem av guttene kom først?* (which of the boys came first?), *hva hendte i går?* (what happened yesterday?), *hva mener du om situasjonen?* (what do you think of the situation?), *hvem har du sendt brevet til?* (to whom have you sent the letter?), *hvem av brødrene sendte du brevet til?* (to which of the brothers did you send the letter?), *hva lever de av?* (what do they live on?).

As will be seen from the above examples the English "which of" about persons is rendered by *hvem av.*

b) *Hvem* is mostly considered a singular pronoun, but can in some connections cover more than one person: *hvem er de to damene der?* (who are those two ladies?), *hvem er syke her i huset?* (who are ill in this house?).

c) The genitive of the interrogative *hvem* is *hvis* (whose): *hvis datter er hun?* (whose daughter is she?), *hvis bok er dette?* (whose book is this?). There is a tendency, however, to avoid this genitive and replace it by verbal or prepositional expressions: *hvem er hun datter av? hvem eier denne boken?*

d) *hvilken (hvilket, hvilke)* corresponding to "which" and "what", and with the same meaning but more colloquial, *hva for en (hva for et, hva for noen),* can be applied as nouns but have primarily an adjectival position; *hva slags* (what kind):

I dag har jeg lest en god bok. Hvilken? or *Hva for en?* (Today I have read a good book. Which one?). *På dette bildet ser jeg tre hus. Hvilket* or *hva for et er ditt?* (On this picture I see three houses. Which one is yours?). *Det er så mange barn på gaten. Hvilke* or *hva for noen er dine?* (There are so many children in the street. Which ones are yours?). *Hvilken* or *hva for en bil er din?* (Which car is yours?), *hvilket* or *hva for et hus bor han i?* (what house does he live in?), *hvilke* or *hva for noen kopper bør jeg kjøpe?* (what cups should I buy?); *hva slags sigaretter røyker De?* (what kind of cigarettes do you smoke?).

e) When the interrogative pronoun is the subject of a dependent clause, it is usually followed by *som:*
   jeg vet ikke hvem som kan gjøre det (I do not know who can do it), *han fortalte meg hvem som hadde gjort det* (he told me who had done it), *spør henne hva som er i veien* (ask her what the trouble is).

f) *hvilken (hvilket, hvilke)* is sometimes used in exclamations where the English has "what a": e. g. *hvilken skjønnhet!* (what a beauty!), *hvilket under!* (what a miracle!), *hvilke rikdommer der er!* (what riches there are!). This usage is rather literary, however, and in less formal language similar exclamations are expressed by means of *for en (for et, for noen): for en tosk jeg har vært* (what a fool I have been), *for et makeløst vær* (what exceptional weather), *for noen fortryllende barn* (what charming children).

INDEFINITE PRONOUNS *(Ubestemte pronomener)*

§ 109. Used as nouns are:

a) *man* (one, you, they) only as subject of the sentence: *man sier at verden blir bedre* (they say, people say, it is said that the world is getting better), *man kan ikke være sikker på resultatet* (one cannot be sure of the result), *man mener i London at situasjonen er noe lysere nå* (they think in London that the situation is somewhat lighter now), *man frykter for at krigen er uunngåelig* (they fear that the war is unavoidable).

b) *en* is often synonymous for *man*, but has a more general scope, thus including the person speaking, and is in more colloquial use: *en kan aldri vite hva som vil hende* (one can never know what will happen), *en får finne seg i kritikk* (one has to put up with criticism). The advantage about *en* is that it can be applied as object, indirect object, in the genitive case and be governed by prepositions: *det er ikke godt å si hva som kan hende en i det landet* (it is not easy to say what may happen to one in that country), *slikt gir en tillit til mennenskene* (such things give one confidence in human beings), *det kan ikke ventes av en at ens hus skal stå åpent for enhver* (it cannot be expected [from one] that one's house [shall] be open to everybody).

c) The following indefinite pronouns can be used both as nouns and adjectives, and they are inflected in gender and number:

Common	Neuter	Plural
noen (some, any, someone, anyone, somebody, anybody)	*noe* (some, any, something, anything)	*noen* (some, any)
ingen (no, no one, nobody, none)	*intet* (no, nothing, none)	*ingen* (no, none)
mang en (many a)	*mangt et* (many a)	*mange* (many)
annen (other)	*annet* (other)	*andre* (other, others)
all (all)	*alt* (all, everything)	*alle* (all)
hver or *enhver* (every, every one, everybody, each, any, any one)	*hvert* or *ethvert* (every, each)	no plural
no form	no form	*få* (few)

d) As will be seen from the above list, the pronoun *noen*, etc. stands for both "some" and "any", which means that it is used in affirmative, negative, interrogative and doubtful statements:
noen kommer (somebody is coming), *jeg skal si deg noe* (I shall tell you something), *han vil ha noen frimerker* (he wants some stamps), *hun bodde i Skottland i noen år* (she lived in Scotland for some years), *kommer det noen?* (is anyone coming?), *hun kunne ikke gi meg noe håp* (she could not give me any hope), *har du noen blyanter?* (do you have any pencils?), *nei, jeg har ikke noen* (no, I do not have any).
The neuter form *noe* is often combined with collective nouns of common gender or plural to signify part or quantity of: *jeg vil ha noe mat* (I want to have some food), *har du noe penger på deg?* (do you have any money on you?).

e) The use of *ingen*, etc.:
ingen adgang (no admittance), *ingen vet hvor han bor* (nobody knows where he lives), *intet menneske er fullkomment* (no human being is perfect), *intet har gledet meg mer* (nothing has given me more pleasure), *han forstod intet av dette* (he understood nothing of this), *dette er ingenmannsland* (this is no man's land).

Instead of *ingen* is often said *ikke noen*. Particularly the neuter *intet* is replaced by *ikke noe* when preceding a noun, and by *ingenting* (nothing) when it has the function of a noun: *vi har ikke noen bil* (we have no car), *ikke noe menneske kan tåle en slik varme* (no human being can stand such heat), *han har ingenting å leve av* (he has nothing to live on).

f) The pronouns *mang en* and *mangt et* emphasize at the same time both the individual and the multitude: *mang en gang* (many a time), *mangt et menneske* (many a person); the plural *mange* corresponds entirely to the English "many".

g) *annen, annet* becomes also *andre* after the definite article *den, det*, especially when the following noun is a concrete: *den andre siden av veien* (the other side of the road), but: *på den annen side* (on the other hand). Cf. § 83.

h) The common gender *all* can only be used in connection with a noun: *all frukt er billig nå* (all fruit is cheap now). The neuter form has also often adjectival function: *alt gullet ble brakt i sikkerhet* (all the gold was carried into safety). In solemn language, especially in biblical style, the pronoun preceding the definite form of the noun renders the English "all the": *all verden skulle innskrives i manntall* (all the world should be taxed [registered]), *alt folket priste Gud* (all the people gave praise unto God). The neuter *alt* can stand alone, as a noun, and mean *everything*, and the plural *alle* meaning *everybody*: *han mistet alt* (he lost everything), *alle kjenner ham* (everybody knows him).

i) As is the case after demonstrative pronouns (see § 103 b and c), the noun often takes the definite form after the plural *alle:* here the same distinction will be made as in English "all" and "all the": *alle forretninger må stenge klokken fem* (all shops must close at five o'clock), *alle forretningene var vakkert dekorert* (all the shops were beautifully decorated).

j) *hver* and *enhver* etc. correspond to both *every* and *each: hver dag* (every day), *hver av guttene fikk et eple* (each of the boys got an apple), *hvert år* (every year). **NB!** *hver tredje time* (every three hours), *hvert tredje år* (every three years).

k) *få* (few) and *noen få* (a few) can of course only be used in the plural.

Conjunctions *(Konjunksjoner)*

The conjunctions are coordinating or subordinating.

§ 110. The **coordinating** conjunctions are as in English:

a) combining: *og* (and), *både – og* (both – and), *så vel – som* (as well – as), *dels – dels* (partly – partly), *for* (for), *ti* (for).

b) disjunctive: *eller* (or), *enten – eller* (either – or), *verken – eller* (neither – nor).

c) adversative: *men* (but).

When combining verbs the *og* often gives the second verb the function of the present participle in English: *han lå og sov* (he lay sleeping), *hun stod og skalv* (she stood trembling). Cf. § 119.

Unlike English, *både – og* can be used even when there are more than two alternatives: *vi dyrker både epler og pærer og plommer* (we grow apples, [and] pears and plums).

§ 111. The **subordinating** conjunctions are:

a) denoting time: *da* ("when", especially referring to an incident completed in the past): *da jeg var i England, besøkte jeg herr Nelson* (when I was in England, I visited Mr. Nelson). – *når* ("when(ever)", referring to what usually happens or happened or what will happen in the future): *når jeg var i England, besøkte jeg herr N.* (whenever I was in England, I visited Mr. N.), *når jeg er i England, besøker jeg alltid herr N.* (whenever I am in England, I always visit Mr. N.), *når jeg kommer til England, vil jeg besøke herr N.* (when I come to England, I will visit Mr. N.). – *etter* or *etter at* (after). – *før* or *førenn* (before, till). – *innen* (before). – *idet* (as, while). – *mens* (while). – *til* or *inntil* (till, until). – *fra* (since). – *siden* (since). – *som* (as). – *så snart som* (as soon as). – *så lenge som* (as long as).

b) denoting cause: *da* (as). – *fordi* (because). – *siden* (since). – *ettersom* (as).

c) denoting condition: *hvis* (if). – *dersom* (if). – *om* (if). – *såfremt* (provided that). – *i fall* (in case). – *uten* (unless). – *med mindre* (unless).

A condition can be expressed just by inversion of the word order (see § 155.)

d) denoting concession: *skjønt* or *enskjønt* (though, although). – *om* or *enda om* or *selv om* (even if).

e) denoting purpose: *for at* (so that). – *så* (so that).

f) denoting consequence: *så at* or *slik at* (so that).

g) denoting comparison: *som* or *liksom* (as). – *så* – *som* or *likså* – *som* (as – as, so – as). – *jo* – *jo* or *jo* – *desto* (the – the). – *enn* (than). – *som om* (as if).

h) in front of noun clauses: *at* (that)*, which can be left out: *jeg hørte (at) han kom* (I heard [that] he came). – *om* (if, whether; not to be mixed up with the conditional conjunction above): *jeg vet ikke om han kommer* (I do not know whether he will come). With regard to that-clauses governed by prepositions, see § 152.

§ 112. **In many cases English has participial constructions where Norwegian has to apply subordinate clauses:** *da han fant situasjonen for vanskelig, solgte han forretningen* (finding the situation too difficult, he sold his business), *da hun hadde skrevet brevet, gikk hun til sengs* (having written the letter, she went to bed), *mens han kjørte bilen, hørte han en merkelig lyd* (while driving his car he heard a strange sound), *i begynnelsen ble kullene kalt sjøkull, fordi de ble ført sjøveien til London* (at first the coals, being carried to London by sea, were called sea-coals), *John ble sendt til Europa, mens hans to brødre ble hjemme* (John was sent to Europe, his two brothers being left at home), *da han var omringet av fiender på alle kanter, gav han opp* (being surrounded by enemies on all sides, he gave up). Cf. §§ 119 and 120.

Verbs *(Verber)*

INFINITIVE, STEM, MOOD *(Infinitiv, stamme, modus)*

§ 113. **The infinitive.** The sign of the infinitive is *å*, corresponding to English "to". **The greater part of the infinitives in Norwegian end in an unstressed -*e*,** which means that the majority of the verbs have at least two syllables: *å være* (to be), *å leve* (to live), *å snakke* (to speak), *å kjøre* (to drive), *å komme* (to come), *å trekke* (to pull), *å skyve* (to push). If we take away the ending -*e*, we get the stem of the verb: *vær, lev, snakk, kjør, kom* (cf. § 6 m), *trekk, skyv.* However, quite a number of verbs are monosyllabic, the infinitive ending in the

---

*) **NB!** Do not confuse this conjunction with the relative pronoun "that" *(som)*. Cp. § 106 a with note.

stressed vowel of the stem: *å le* (to laugh), *å ta* (to take), *å snu* (to turn), *å tro* (to believe), *å stå* (to stand), *å gå* (to go), *å slå* (to beat, to strike).

The same stress is preserved in many compounds with the prefix *for-* and *be-*: e. g. *forstå* (understand), *forgå* (perish), *forslå* (suffice), *bestå* (consist), *begå* (commit). With other prefixes the stress is transferred to the first syllable: e. g. *tilta* (increase), *avse* (spend), *foreslå* (propose), *angå* (concern).

For infinitive after prepositions see § 151.

§ 114. The verb has three **moods**, viz. imperative, subjunctive and indicative.

§ 115. **The imperative is always like the stem of the verb** (§ 113): e. g. *skyv* (push), *trekk* (pull), *kjør til høyre* (drive to the right), *vent på summetonen* (wait for the dial tone), *gå på fortauet* (walk on the footway). A doubled consonant is preserved: e. g. *snakk høyt* (speak aloud); but *mm* becomes *m* only: e. g. *kom inn* (come in). (Cf. § 6 *m*.) Also *rr* is sometimes reduced to a single: e. g. *spør* or *spørr* from *spørre* (ask).

§ 116. **The subjunctive mood occurs only in the present tense and has the same form as the infinitive.** It is comparatively rare in Norwegian, and is only used in expressions with optative or concessive meaning.

Examples:

Lenge leve Kongen or *Kongen lenge leve* – long live the King
Gud bevare Kongen og fedrelandet – God save the King and the
country
Gud velsigne deg – God bless you
Ære være Gud – glory be to God
Skje din vilje – Thy will be done
Det koste hva det vil – it may cost ever so much, i. e. at all hazards
Jeg gir ham den ikke, han være   I do not give it to him, be he
aldri så mye min bror   ever so much my brother

§ 117. The **indicative** mood appears in the active and passive voices, and in various tenses, simple and compound forms. The compound forms are used in tenses outside the present tense and the past tense.

ACTIVE VOICE *(Aktiv)*

§ 118. **The present tense of nearly all verbs is made by adding *-r* to the infinitive, and this ending is independent of person or number:** *kjører, snakker, venter, trekker, skyver, ler, tar, tror, går, forstår, begår, tiltar, avser.*

57

These forms render also the continuous forms in English, "am (is, are) driving, speaking" etc. (See §§ 139 and 140). There are very few exceptions to this formation of the present tense: *er* (of *være*, be), *gjør* (of *gjøre*, do, make), *spør* (of *spørre*, ask), *vet* (of *vite*, know), and the modal auxiliaries *kan, skal, vil, må, bør, tør* (see § 128).

PASSIVE VOICE *(Passiv)*

See §§ 129–133.

PARTICIPLES *(Partisipper)*

§ 119. The **present participle** is formed by adding -*ende* to the stem of the verb: e. g. *vær/ende, lev/ende, snakk/ende, skriv/ende, komm/ende, le/ende, tro/ende, stå/ende* etc.

The present participle is mainly used attributively as adjective and as adverb: *en lovende kunstner* (a promising artist), *blinkende stjerner* (twinkling stars), *et dansende barn* (a dancing child), *han snakker flytende* (he speaks fluently).

In appositive use it has a much more limited scope than it has in English. As seen above, that construction is often rendered by conjunctions (§§ 110 and 112) or relative clauses: e. g. *mannen som visste at datteren hadde glemt nøkkelen, låste ikke døren* (the man, knowing that his daughter had forgotten the key, did not lock the door).

The participle is often, as in English, used after the verbs *komme* (come) in order to indicate an accompanying activity: *han kom syngende nedover gaten* (he came singing down the street). Sometimes it is also used after the verb *bli* (remain): *han ble liggende på marken* (he remained lying on the ground).

With regard to the inflection and the comparison of the participles see §§ 44 a, f, 47 b, 48, 49, 70.

§ 120. The **past participle** is used to form the compound tenses perfect (§ 136) and pluperfect (§ 137) and the periphrastic passive voice after the auxiliary verb *bli* (§§ 129–133). It is often applied attributively as an adjective and as an adverb: *en brukt bil* (a used car), *bortkastede penger* (wasted money), *et uventet godt resultat* (an unexpectedly good result).

Like the present participle also the past participle in appositive use is mostly replaced by subordinate (§ 112) and relative clauses: *pioner er et navn som ble gitt til de første emigranter* (pioneer is a name given to the first emigrants), *en annen plan som ble fremsatt samme år, var å bygge en tunnel* (another plan set forth in the same year, was to build a tunnel).

The past participles vary in form according to the different classes of verbs. In the list of strong verbs below (§ 122) all the participles are given, and in the case of weak verbs the formation of the participles are explained under each group (§§ 124–128).

STRONG AND WEAK VERBS *(Sterke og svake verber)*

§ 121. An important distinction is made between strong verbs and weak verbs.

§ 122. A strong (or irregular) verb has no ending in the past tense, but most of them change the vowel and also present the same or another mutation in the past participle.

The strong verbs are listed below in alphabetic order. Also a couple of weak verbs are included in the list because they are characterized by a similar irregularity in the past tense. Most of them are frequently used in Norwegian, a fact that accounts for their keeping up an irregular conjugation.

Infinitive	Past tense	Past participle
adlyde (obey)	*adlød*	*adlydt*
be (pray, ask, beg)	*ba(d)*	*bedt*
bedra (deceive)	*bedro(g)*	*bedradd* or *bedratt*
* *begrave* (bury)	*begrov*	*begravd*
begripe (comprehend)	*begrep*	*begrepet*
beholde (keep, retain)	*beholdt*	*beholdt*
binde (bind, tie)	*bandt*	*bundet*
bite (bite)	*bet*	*bitt*
bli (become, remain, stay, be)	*ble*	*blitt*
brekke (break)	*brakk*	*brukket*
brenne (burn)	*brant*	*brent* (intr.)
breste or *briste* (burst)	*brast*	*bristet* or *brusted*
bryte (break)	*brøt*	*brutt*
by or *byde* (order, bid, offer)	*bød*	*budt*
bære (carry, bear, wear)	*bar*	*båret*
dra (pull, draw, drag)	*dro(g)*	*dradd* or *dratt*
drikke (drink)	*drakk*	*drukket*
drive (drive, compel, saunter)	*drev*	*drevet*
ete (eat)	*åt*	*ett*
falle (fall, drop)	*falt*	*falt*

Infinitive	Past tense	Past participle
fare (go, travel)	*for*	*far(e)t*
finne (find)	*fant*	*funnet*
fly (fly)	*fløy*	*fløyet*
flyte (flow, float)	*fløt*	*flytt*
forby (forbid, prohibit)	*forbød*	*forbudt*
fordrive (expel)	*fordrev*	*fordrevet*
forlate (leave)	*forlot*	*forlatt*
fornemme (feel, perceive)	*fornam*	*fornummet*
forstå (understand)	*forsto(d)*	*forstått*
forsvinne (disappear)	*forsvant*	*forsvunnet*
fryse (be cold, freeze)	*frøs*	*frosset* (intr.)
fyke (drift)	*føk*	*føket*
få (get, receive)	*fikk*	*fått*
* *gale* (crow)	*gol*	*galt*
gi (give)	*ga(v)*	*gitt*
gidde (take the trouble, care)	*gadd*	*giddet*
gjelde (concern)	*gjaldt*	*gjeldt*
gli (slide, glide)	*gled*	*glidd*
glippe (fail, slip)	*glapp*	*glippet*
* *gnage* (gnaw, chafe, fret)	*gnog*	*gnaget*
* *gnelle* (shriek, shrill)	*gnall*	*gnelt*
* *gni* (rub)	*gned*	*gnidd*
* *grave* (dig)	*grov*	*gravd*
* *grine* (fret, be cross)	*grein*	*grint*
gripe (grasp, seize)	*grep*	*grepet*
gråte (weep)	*gråt*	*grått*
* *gyse* (shudder)	*gjøs*	*gyst*
* *gyte* (spawn, pour)	*gjøt*	*gytt*
gyve (fly, rush)	*gjøv*	*gjøvet*
gå (go, walk)	*gikk*	*gått*
henge (hang)	*hang*	*hengt* (intr.)
* *hete* (be called)	*het*	*hett*
* *hive* (throw, heave)	*he(i)v*	*hivd*
hjelpe (help)	*hjalp*	*hjulpet*
* *hogge* (cut, chop, hew)	*hogg*	*hogd*
holde (keep, hold)	*holdt*	*holdt*
* *hugge* (cut, hew)	*hugg*	*hugd*
* *hvine* (shriek)	*hven*	*hvint*
klinge (sound)	*klang*	*kling(e)t*
* *klyve* (climb)	*kløv*	*kløvet*
knekke (crack, break)	*knakk*	*knek(ke)t* (intr.)
knipe (pinch, catch)	*knep*	*knepet*

Infinitive	Past tense	Past participle
komme (come)	*kom*	*kommet*
krype (creep)	*krøp*	*krøpet*
kvede (sing, chant)	*kvad*	*kvedet*
kvekke (start, jump)	*kvakk*	*kvekket*
kveppe (start, jump)	*kvapp*	*kveppet*
* *kvine* (shriek)	*kvein*	*kvint*
la(te) (let)	*lot*	*latt*
le (laugh)	*lo*	*ledd*
legge (lay)	*la*	*lagt* (actually a weak verb, where the ending in the past tense has been dropped *(lagde)*, and with change of the vowel *a* to *e* in the infinitive and the present tense)

* *lekke* (leak)	*lakk*	*lek(ke)t*
* *li* (pass)	*led*	*lidd*
* *lide* or *li* (suffer, endure)	*led*	*lidt* or *lidd*
ligge (lie)	*lå*	*ligget*
* *lyde* (sound, run, obey)	*lød*	*lydt*
lyve (lie, tell a lie)	*løy*	*løyet*
løpe (run)	*løp*	*løpt*
* *male* (grind, pur)	*mol*	*malt*
* *nyse* (sneeze)	*nøs*	*nyst*
nyte (enjoy)	*nøt*	*nytt*
overvære (attend)	*overvar*	*overvært*
pipe (pipe, whistle)	*pep*	*pepet*
* *reke* (drift, idle, stray)	*rak*	*rekt*
rekke (reach, suffice, last)	*rakk*	*rukket*
renne (run, flow)	*rant*	*rent* (intr.)
* *ri* or *ride* (ride)	*red*	*ridd*
rinne (run, flow)	*rant*	*runnet*
rive (tear)	*rev*	*revet*
ryke (smoke, break, burst)	*røk*	*røket*
se (see, look)	*så*	*sett*
si (say)	*sa*	*sagt* (actually a weak verb, where the ending in the past tense has been dropped *(sagde)*, and with change of vowel in the infinitive and the present tense *(sier)*.

Infinitive	Past tense	Past participle
sige (sink slowly)	*seig*	*seget*
sitte (sit)	*satt*	*sittet*
* *skinne* (shine)	*skjen* or *skein*	*skint*
skjelve (shiver, tremble)	*skalv*	*skjelvet*
skjære (cut)	*skar*	*skåret*
skrelle (clang, rattle)	*skrall*	*skrelt* (intr.)
skride (proceed)	*skred*	*skredet*
skrike (cry, scream)	*skrek*	*skreket*
skrive (write)	*skrev*	*skrevet*
* *skryte* (brag, boast)	*skrøt*	*skrytt*
skvette (start, give a sudden start, splash)	*skvatt*	*skvettet* (intr.)
skyte (shoot, fire)	*skjøt*	*skutt*
skyve (push)	*skjøv*	*skjøvet*
slenge (dangle, idle)	*slang*	*slengt* (intr.)
* *sleppe* (drop, let go)	*slapp*	*sloppet*
slippe (drop, avoid)	*slapp*	*sloppet*
slite (wear out, toil)	*slet*	*slitt*
slå (strike, beat)	*slo*	*slått*
slåss (fight)	*sloss*	*slåss* (actually a passive form, and therefore just *slåss* in the present tense. Cf. § 132).
smelle (clap, bang, crack)	*smalt*	*smelt* (intr.)
smette (pass, slip)	*smatt*	*smettet*
smyge (sneak)	*smøg*	*smøget*
snike (sneak)	*snek*	*sneket*
* *snyte* (blow one's nose, cheat)	*snøt*	*snytt*
sove (sleep)	*sov*	*sovet*
spinne (spin)	*spant*	*spunnet*
sprekke (crack, burst)	*sprakk*	*sprukket*
sprette (leap, bounce)	*spratt*	*sprettet* (intr.)
springe (jump, run, blow up)	*sprang*	*sprunget*
stige (increase)	*steg*	*steget*
stikke (sting, put)	*stakk*	*stukket*
stjele (steal)	*stjal*	*stjålet*
strekke (stretch, suffice)	*strakk*	*strukket*
* *stride* or *stri* (strive, struggle)	*stred*	*stridd*
stryke (stroke, iron, fail)	*strøk*	*strøket*
støkke (start, give a sudden start)	*stokk*	*støk(ke)t*
stå (stand)	*sto(d)*	*stått*
svelte (starve)	*svalt*	*sveltet*

Infinitive	Past tense	Past participle
* *sverge* (swear)	*svor*	*svoret*
* *svi* (smart, pain, singe)	*sved* or *svei*	*svidd*
svike (deceive, defraud)	*svek*	*sveket*
* *svinge* (swing, soar)	*svang*	*svunget* or *sving(e)t*
svinne (vanish, shrink)	*svant*	*svunnet*
svive (spin round, ramble)	*sveiv*	*svivd*
synge (sing)	*sang*	*sunget*
synke (sink)	*sank*	*sunket*
ta (take)	*tok*	*tatt*
treffe (meet, hit)	*traff*	*truffet*
trekke (pull, draw, drag)	*trakk*	*trukket*
trive (catch, clutch, grasp)	*treiv*	*trevet*
tvinge (compel, force)	*tvang*	*tvunget*
tyte (filter, ooze)	*tøt*	*tytt*
vekke (start, give a start)	*vakk*	*vekket* (intr.)
vike (yield, give way)	*vek*	*veket* (intr.)
vinde (wind)	*vandt*	*vundet*
vinne (win)	*vant*	*vunnet*
* *vri* (twist)	*vred*	*vridd*
være (be)	*var*	*vært*

All the verbs marked with * have more and more adopted weak conjugation. The verbs marked (intr.) have strong conjugation when they are used intransitively. When they take, or can take, object, they have weak (regular) conjugation. Thus the difference between *huset brant ned* (the house burnt down) – *han brente ned huset* (he burnt down the house), *vannet skvatt til alle kanter* (the water splashed in all directions) – *han skvettet vann på oss* (he splashed water on us).

§ 123. **All other verbs than those listed above, are weak or regular verbs, the chief criterion of which is that they have a dental ending *(d* or *t)* in the past tense and the past participle.** Thus by far the greatest number of Norwegian verbs are regular verbs.

§ 124. a) The primary ending of a weak verb is *-de* in the past tense and *-d* in the past participle. This is still the case with verbs where the stem ends in a diphthong or in a *g* or *v* after a vowel, or in a *d* after a diphthong:

eie (own)	*eide*	*eid*
suge (suck)	*sugde*	*sugd*
leve (live)	*levde*	*levd*
arbeide (work)	*arbeidde*	*arbeidd*
	(or *arbeidet*)	(or *arbeidet*) Cf. § 126

63

b) A double *g* in the stem is reduced to a single consonant before the dental:

bygge (build)   *bygde*   *bygd*

c) Originally both *si* (say) and *legge* (lay) belong to this class, but owing to their irregular conjugation they have been listed under irregular or strong verbs (see § 122).

d) A couple of verbs may preserve an original *g* of the stem in the past tense and the past participle:

vie (consecrate, wed) *vigde* (or *viet*)   *vigd* (or *viet*)
                                                Cf. § 126 b

e) **NB**! To this class also belongs:

gjøre (do, make)   *gjorde*   *gjort* Cf. § 118

§ 125. a) After *m, n, nd, ng, k, l, ld, p, r, s*, and a single *t* preceded by a vowel the ending in the past tense will be *-te* and in the past participle *-t*:

glemme (forget)	*glemte*	*glemt*
låne (borrow, lend)	*lånte*	*lånt*
sende (send)	*sendte*	*sendt*
stenge (close)	*stengte*	*stengt*
leke (play)	*lekte*	*lekt*
hvile (rest)	*hvilte*	*hvilt*
melde (inform, report)	*meldte*	*meldt*
kjøpe (buy)	*kjøpte*	*kjøpt*
kjøre (drive)	*kjørte*	*kjørt*
reise (go, travel)	*reiste*	*reist*
lete (search)	*lette*	*lett*

As will be seen from the verb *glemme*, also in this group a double consonant is reduced (cf. § 124 b). Other examples are:

kjenne (know, feel)	*kjente*	*kjent*
kalle (call)	*kalte*	*kalt*
dekke (cover)	*dekte*	*dekt*

b) With change of vowel in the past tense and the past participle, and in some cases other irregularities too:

bringe (bring)	*brakte*	*brakt*
dølge (conceal)	*dulte*	*dult*
fortelle (tell)	*fortalte*	*fortalt*
følge (follow, accompany)	*fulgte*	*fulgt*
kvele (choke, strangle)	*kvalte*	*kvalt*

rekke (hand, pass, stretch)	*rakte*	*rakt*
selge (sell)	*solgte*	*solgt*
sette (set, place)	*satte*	*satt*
smøre (smear, lubricate)	*smurte*	*smurt*
strekke (stretch)	*strakte*	*strakt*
telle (count)	*talte* or *telte*	*talt* or *telt*
tre (tread, step)	*trådte*	*trådt*
vekke (arouse)	*vakte*	*vakt* (but *vekte, vekt* in the meaning *awake*)
velge (chose, elect)	*valgte*	*valgt*

c) **NB!** With no ending in the present tense (cf. § 118):

spørre (ask)	*spurte*	*spurt* (pres. *spør*)
vite (know)	*visste*	*visst* (pres. *vet*)

(In the latter verb the *s* is geminated in the past tense and the past participle in order to avoid confusion with the verb *vise* (show) – *viste* – *vist* (cf. § 42 b).

§ 126. a) Many verbs have an ending of the stem that makes both the endings *-de*, *-d* and *-te*, *-t* hard to pronounce, and therefore the ending *-et* is applied both in the past tense and the past participle. One will easily hear that this conjugation is necessary in verbs with the post-consonant endings *-ge*, *-ke*, *-le*, *-ne*, *-re*, *-se*, *-te* in the infinitive:

verge (defend)	*verget*	*verget*
huske (remember)	*husket*	*husket*
veksle (change, exchange)	*vekslet*	*vekslet*
åpne (open)	*åpnet*	*åpnet*
angre (repent)	*angret*	*angret*
danse (dance)	*danset*	*danset*
koste (cost)	*kostet*	*kostet*

b) To this class belong some verbs where the infinitive ends in *-e* after a vowel:

true (threaten)	*truet*	*truet*
skye (cloud)	*skyet*	*skyet*

c) Also some verbs where the stem ends in *b*, *g* or a pronounced *d* after a vowel: e. g. *klebe* (stick, paste), *lage* (make), *bade* (bathe, swim). Further a group of verbs that end in *-je* after a consonant: *ferje* (ferry), *herje* (harry, devastate).

Most verbs of this class may take the ending *-a* instead of *-et* in the past tense and the past participle, especially in a broadly popular style.

§ 127. Verbs that end in the vowel of the stem, which of course is stressed, add *-dde* in the past tense and *-dd* in the past participle:

tro (believe, think)	*trodde*	*trodd*
snu (turn)	*snudde*	*snudd*
sy (sew)	*sydde*	*sydd*
fø (feed)	*fødde*	*fødd*
skje (happen)	*skjedde*	*skjedd*

With irregular past participle:

ha (have)	*hadde*	*hatt*

With irregular past tense:

dø (die) *døde* *dødd* (Instead of the participle *dødd* is ordinarily used the adjective *død:* e. g. *han er død* [he has died] instead of *han har dødd*)

AUXILIARY VERBS *(Hjelpeverber)*

§ 128. a) The verbs *ha* (have), *være* (be) and *bli* (be) are used as auxiliaries in order to make compound tenses or express the passive voice (see § 130). In addition there are the following modal auxiliaries, all of which, unlike English, can be used in the infinitive and past participle and accordingly form part of the compound tenses: future, perfect and pluperfect.

Infinitive	Present tense	Past tense	Past participle
å kunne (to be able to)	*kan* (can)	*kunne* (could)	*kunnet*
å skulle (to be going to)	*skal* (shall)	*skulle* (should)	*skullet*
å ville (to be willing to)	*vil* (will)	*ville* (would)	*villet*
å måtte (to have to)	*må* (must)	*måtte* (must)	*måttet*
å burde	*bør* (ought to)	*burde* (ought to)	*burdet*
å tore (dare to)	*tør* (dare)	*torde* (dared)	*tort*

b) **After the modal auxiliaries the principal verb is always in the infinitive:** *jeg vil skrive* (I will write), *du skal ikke stjele* (you shall not steal), *vi måtte reise med fly* (we had to travel by plane), *jeg har ikke tort si det til noen* (I have not dared to say it to anybody), *man kan aldri vite* (one can never tell), *jeg sa han burde kjøpe en ny dress* (I said he ought to buy a new suit).

c) After an auxiliary verb a completing principal verb denoting motion from one place to another can be left out: e. g. *jeg må (gå) hjem* (I must go home), *han skal (reise) til England i juli* (he will go to England in July). Cf. Shakespeare: I must to Corinth.

d) The auxiliary *skal, skulle* also renders the English **am (are, is) to be:** *båten skal gå innom Bergen* (the ship is to call at Bergen), and **be about to:** *vi skal nettopp spise frokost nå* (we are just about to have breakfast now).

e) Also *få* can be used as an auxiliary verb, with the meaning "may", often combined with *må* or *kan*: e. g. *får jeg* (or *må jeg få*) *presentere* (may I introduce), *får jeg* (or *kan jeg få*) *snakke med* (may I speak with).

PASSIVE VOICE *(Passiv)*

The passive voice is expressed in two ways.

§ 129. The one which can only be applied in the infinitive (and then also in the future tense), the present tense, and, more rarely, in the past tense, is formed **by the addition of -s to the respective active forms,** the present tense, however, dropping the *-r*. Compare the following active and passive voices: *å tenne* (to turn on, viz. light) – *å tennes* (to be turned on), *vi skal tenne lysene* (we shall turn on the lights) – *lysene vil tennes* (the lights will be turned on), *jeg tenner lysene* (I turn on the lights) – *lysene tennes* (the lights are turned on), *jeg tente lysene* (I turned on the lights) – *lysene tentes* (the lights were turned on).

§ 130. The other way of making passive is to apply the periphrastic form, being expressed **by means of the auxiliary verb *bli*** (be) **plus the past participle of the principal verb:** *å bli tent* (to be turned on), *lysene blir tent* (the lights are turned on), *lysene ble tent* (the lights were turned on). This formation of the passive can be used in all tenses; in the perfect tense (cf. § 136): *lysene har blitt tent* (the lights have been turned on), in the pluperfect (cf. § 137): *lysene hadde blitt tent* (the lights had been turned on), in the future: *lysene vil bli tent* (the lights will be turned on).

§ 131. In the perfect (§ 136) and the pluperfect (§ 137) the auxiliary verb *være* is often used instead of *ha*, and then the participle *blitt* can be left out: *lysene er (blitt) tent* (the lights have been turned on); *lysene var (blitt) tent* (the lights had been turned on).

§ 132. Some verbs appear in passive form but with active meaning. They are called deponent verbs and are also applicable in the past participle. Such verbs are:

Infinitive	Present tense	Past tense	Past participle
finnes (exist, be)	*finnes* or *fins*	*fantes* or *fans*	*har funnes*
eldes (grow old)	*eldes*	*eldedes*	» *eldes*
minnes (remember)	*minnes*	*mintes*	» *min(n)es*
lykkes (succeed)	*lykkes*	*lyktes*	» *lykkes*
synes (appear, think)	*synes* or *syns*	*syntes*	» *syn(e)s*
trives (thrive)	*trives*	*trivdes*	» *triv(e)s*
slåss (fight)	*slåss*	*sloss*	» *slåss*

Note that the verb *lykkes* (succeed) usually takes an impersonal construction in Norwegian: *det lyktes meg å få en billett* (I succeeded in getting a ticket). **NB**! The verb *synes* has the meaning "have the impression": *jeg synes Oslo er en pen by* (I think, my impression is, that Oslo is a nice city). The verb *tro* (think, believe) indicates that one has not had the opportunity of founding a personal judgement: *jeg tror at Oslo er en pen by* (I think that Oslo is a nice city, as far as I know, may conclude).

§ 133. The passive *s*-construction has a rather formal character, and is mostly found when a general statement is given, whereas the periphrastic form more implies a finished action. That explains why the *s*-form is most easily applied in the infinitive and the present tense; compare the following sentences:
Fjellet kan ses på lang avstand (the mountain can be seen at a long distance) – *morderen ble sett utenfor hovedstaden i går* (the murderer was seen outside the capital yesterday); *blomstene selges til inntekt for Røde Kors* (the flowers are sold for the benefit of the Red Cross) – *huset blir antagelig solgt i dag* (the house will probably be sold to-day).
That is the reason why the *s*-form is so commonly used in instructions, rules and regulations of general appeal: *et egg bør kokes i minst tre minutter* (an egg ought to be boiled for at least three minutes), *billetter løses ved inngangen* (tickets are bought at the entrance), *slike erstatninger utbetales sjelden* (such compensations are rarely made), *flagget fires ved solnedgang* (the flag is lowered at sunset).

The brief and striking form of the *s*-passive makes it very applicable in advertisements and newspaper articles, especially in headlines: *brukte biler selges* (used cars for sale), *sko repareres på dagen* (shoes promptly repaired), *værelse ønskes* (rooms wanted), *Stortinget åpnes i dag* (the Storting is opened to-day), *dødsstraffen oppheves i landet* (capital punishment is done away with in the country).

In many cases the *s*-passive is advantageously avoided by the changing of the construction into the active voice. Compare: *vikar søkes* (substitute wanted) – *jeg søker vikar* (I want a substitute); *værelse ønskes* (room wanted) – *ung mann ønsker værelse* (a young man wants a room), *utstillingen åpnes i dag* (the exhibition is opened to-day) – *utstillingen åpner i dag* (the exhibition opens to-day); *billetter løses ved inngangen* (tickets are bought at the entrance) – *man kan løse billetter ved inngangen* (one can buy tickets at the entrance).

TENSES *(Tider)*

§ 134. a) The **present tense** is often employed with future meaning, when this becomes apparent from the context: *han reiser i morgen* (he will leave tomorrow), *det blir snart mørkt* (it will soon get dark), *han blir sendt tilbake om en uke* (he will be sent back in a week).

b) About persons who are still living, it is usual to apply the present tense to state when or where they were born: *jeg er født i Oslo* (I was born in Oslo), *min bror er født i 1936* (my brother was born in 1936). If I want to stress that the person is not alive any longer, the past tense must be used: *min stakkars bror ble født under den første verdenskrigen* (my poor brother was born during the first world war).

§ 135. The **past tense** is sometimes used to express a present feeling: *det var hyggelig å hilse på Dem* (it is nice to see you), *dette var en deilig te* (this is a good tea).

§ 136. The **perfect tense** is formed
a) in the active voice by the present tense of the auxiliary *ha* (have) plus the past participle of the principal verb. The present tense of the auxiliary *være* (be) can be used instead of *ha* when the principal verb is *bli* (become, get, turn, grow) or a verb denoting motion (cf. § 137):
vi har kjøpt et hus (we have bought a house), *har du sett ham?* (have you seen him?), *hun har* (or *er*) *blitt blek* (she has become pale), *han har* (or *er*) *reist til Shanghai* (he has gone to Shanghai), *har* (or *er*) *du alt kommet hjem?* (have you come home already?).

b) in the passive voice (see §§ 130 and 131) by the present tense of the auxiliary *ha* or *være* plus the past participle of the auxiliary *bli* (be) plus the past participle of the principal verb:
*han har (*or *er) blitt glemt* (he has been forgotten), *har* (or *er) telegrammet blitt sendt* (has the telegram been sent?). Cf. § 131.

§ 137. The **pluperfect tense** is formed by means of the past tense of the verb *ha* plus the past participle of the principal verb. The past tense of the auxiliary *være* can be used instead of *ha* when the principal verb is *bli* or a verb denoting motion (cf. above § 136 a):
vi hadde kjøpt et hus (we had bought a house), *hadde du sett ham?* (had you seen him?), *hun hadde* (or *var) blitt blek* (she had become pale), *han hadde* (or *var) reist til Shanghai* (he had gone to Shanghai), *hadde* (or *var) du alt kommet hjem* (had you come home already?), *han hadde* (or *var) blitt glemt* (he had been forgotten), *hadde* (or *var) telegrammet blitt sendt?* (had the telegram been sent?). Cf. § 131.

§ 138. The **future** is expressed in different ways:

a) by the present tense, see above § 134 a.

b) by means of *skal* (shall) and *vil* (will) plus the infinitive of the principal verb. The distinction between *skal* and *vil* is to some extent the same as in English, so that the former is used in the 1st person singular and plural, the latter in the 2nd and 3rd persons singular and plural.
jeg skal reise i morgen (I shall leave to-morrow), *ingen vet hva som vil hende i fremtiden* (nobody knows what will happen in the future).

c) by means of *komme til å* plus the infinitive of the principal verb: *jeg kommer til å reise i morgen* (I shall leave to-morrow), *ingen vet hva som kommer til å hende i fremtiden* (nobody knows what is going to happen in the future).

d) by means of *får* (get) plus the past participle of the principal verb, especially about an action completed in the future: *jeg skal kjøpe bil når jeg får solgt huset* (I shall by a car when I have sold the house).

§ 139. **The continuous form in English, being expressed by the auxiliary "be" plus the present participle of the principal verb, has no special equivalent in Norwegian.** "He is sitting on a chair" is rendered by *Han sitter på en stol*. Other examples are:
hva gjør du i Norge? (what are you doing in Norway?), *hun skrev et langt brev på maskinen* (she was writing a long letter on the type-

writer), *jeg vet ikke hva han har gjort i det siste* (I do not know what he has been doing lately), *går du på kino i kveld?* (are you going to the cinema to-night?).

§ 140. If we want to emphasize that the action is in progress, we sometimes express that by *holde på (med) å* or *være i ferd med å* or *sitte (ligge, stå) og: hun holder på å skrive en bok om Stephenson* (she is writing a book on S.), *jeg har holdt på med å male huset mitt i dag* (I have been painting my house to-day), *vi var akkurat i ferd med å pakke opp koffertene* (we were just unpacking the suitcases), *vi satt og spiste middag* (we were having dinner).

Adverbs *(Adverber)*

§ 141. Adverbs comprise a long list of indeclinable words denoting time, place, degree, manner, etc. Such words are *nå* (now), *alltid* (always), *siden* (later), *her* (here), *ut* (out), *hvor* (where), *særdeles* (particularly), *veldig* (enormously), *således* (thus), *hvorledes* (how), *hvor* (how), *bare* (only).

§ 142. **A few adverbs which indicate direction or motion to a place, can assume the meaning of being at a place when -*e* is added:**

Han gikk bort (hjem, inn, ned, opp, ut) = he went away (home, in, down, up, out).
Han er borte (hjemme, inne, nede, oppe, ute) = he is away (at home, in, down, up, out).

§ 143. **In many instances the neuter form of the corresponding adjective is used as an adverb, thus having the function of the ending "-ly" in English.** Compare the following phrases:

Adjective:	Adverb:
*han har en **pen** håndskrift* (he has a nice handwriting)	*han skriver **pent*** (he writes nicely)
*veien er **lang*** (the way is long)	*vi gikk **langt*** (we went far)
*han spiller en **langsom** vals* (he plays a slow waltz)	*han spiller valsen **langsomt*** (he plays the waltz slowly)

71

det var en stygg spøk (that was a bad joke)	*han behandlet henne stygt* (he treated her badly)
jeg hørte en bitter gråt (I heard a bitter cry)	*hun gråt bittert* (she cried bitterly)
dette er en god bok (this is a good book)	*denne boken er godt skrevet* (this book is well written)
de lever et lykkelig ekteskap (they live a happy marriage)	*de er lykkelig gift* (they are happily married) Cp. § 44 c.
hennes sang er strålende (her singing is wonderful)	*hun synger strålende* (she sings wonderfully) Cp. § 44 f.

§ 144. The adverb *meget* stands for both "very" and "much": e. g. *han er meget rik* (he is very rich), *han er meget rikere enn meg* (he is much richer than I). The form *mye*, which tends to be a bit more informal, renders only "much": e. g. *han er mye eldre enn meg* (he is much older than I), *han reiser mye rundt i landet* (he travels much around in the country). In both these examples also *meget* is applied. The use of *much* before a past participle can only be rendered by *meget*, not *mye*: e. g. *meget forbauset* (much astonished), *planen er blitt meget forandret* (the plan has been much changed), *jeg er Dem meget forbunden* (I am much obliged to you). A combination of *meget* and *mye* like English "very much" is not possible in Norwegian. This English expression has as its equivalents *svært meget (mye)*, *veldig meget (mye)*.

§ 145. Adverbs having the same form as the neuter of the adjectives are susceptible of comparison, and the comparative and superlative are usually like those of the corresponding adjectives:

pent (nicely)	*penere*	*penest*
langsomt (slowly)	*langsommere*	*langsomst*
stygt (badly)	*styggere*	*styggest*
lykkelig (happily)	*lykkeligere*	*lykkeligst*
langt (far) **NB!** *lenger*		*lengst*

§ 146. Adverbs are compared by means of *mer* and *mest* where the corresponding adjectives would require that construction (cf. § 70):

strålende (brilliantly)	*mer strålende*	*mest strålende*

§ 147. A few other adverbs, which are not derived from adjectives, are also subject to comparison:

ofte (often, frequently)	*oftere*	*oftest*
titt (often, frequently)	*tiere*	*tiest*
lenge (long, long time)	*lenger*	*lengst*
gjerne (willingly)	*heller*	*helst*
vel or *godt* (well)	*bedre*	*best*

§ 148. The unstressed adverbs *da, jo, nok, nå, vel* express mostly some modification or mitigation of statement, almost like "indeed", "really", "you know", "supposedly": *hvor gammel er du da?* (how old might you be?), *du er jo blitt professor* (indeed, you have become a professor), *han er nok ikke hjemme* (he is not at home, I am afraid), *det er nå ikke helt sant da* (that is not quite true, you know), *jeg finner vel veien selv* (I shall find the way myself, I presume).

§ 149. For the position of adverbs in a sentence see §§ 156–169.

Prepositions *(Preposisjoner)*

§ 150. Generally speaking each Norwegian preposition has its primary counterpart in English. There are, however, many divergencies in this respect, and on the whole it is hard to give definite rules as to their usage. Below are listed the prepositions with their principal meaning or meanings:

av 1. "of": *en av mine venner* (one of my friends), *uavhengig av* (independent of); nouns denoting quantity and ordinal numbers in connection with dates are not followed by a preposition corresponding to "of": e. g. *en flaske melk* (a bottle of milk), *et par sko* (a pair of shoes), *et par dager* (a couple of days), *den syttende mai* (the seventeenth of May); 2. "by", expressing the agent in the passive voice: *dampmaskinen ble oppfunnet av James Watt* (the steam engine was invented by James Watt); 3. "for", "on account of": *hun gråt av glede* (she wept for joy); 4. "from", "out of": *jeg forstod dette av hans brev* (I understood this from his letter); 5. "on": *avhengig av* (dependent on).

bak or *bakom* – "behind".

blant or *iblant* – "among".

bortenfor – "beyond".

etter (often spelt *efter*) 1. "after": *etter middag* (after dinner); 2. "for" (in search of, expressing something wanted): *jeg ser etter min bok* (I am looking for my book), *hun lengter etter sin mann* (she is longing for her husband); 3. "by", in conformity with: *vi har våre regler å gå etter* (we have our rules to go by).

for 1. "for": *gjør det for meg* (do it for me); 2. "by", in the phrase: *han bor for seg selv* (he lives by himself); 3. "of", in the combination: *i stedet for* or *istedenfor* (instead of, in the place of); *jeg er redd for ham* (I am afraid of him); 4. "to": *jeg ble presentert for ham* (I was introduced to him), *jeg foretrekker te for kaffe* (I prefer tea to coffee).

Note: *for – siden* (ago) and *for – skyld* (for – sake): *han kom hit for ti år siden* (he came here ten years ago), *hun gjorde det for sine barns skyld* (she did it for her children's sake).
In front of an infinitive *for* means "in order to": *han har kommet til Norge for å studere Ibsens dramaer* (he has come to Norway in order to study Ibsen's dramas).

foran – "in front of".

fra – "from".

før 1. "before": *før krigen* (before the war); 2. "till" (in negative expressions): *han kom ikke før mandag* (he did not come till Monday).

gjennom or ***igjennom*** – "through".

hos 1. "with", in one's company: *jeg bor hos mine foreldre* (I live with my parents); 2. "at", in one's house: *jeg har vært hos skomakeren* (I have been at the shoemaker's).

i 1. "in": *i Norge* (in Norway), *i Oslo* (in Oslo); 2. "at", in connection with names of towns, streets: *i Tønsberg* (at Tønsberg), *i Ullevål Hageby* (at Ullevål Hageby), *i Kongens gate 15* (at 15 King's Road); 3. "for", about length of time: *i mange år* (for several years); 4. "during", in the course of: *i de siste årene av krigen bodde han i Sverige* (during the last years of the war he lived in Sweden); 5. "to": *gå i kirken* (go to church).
The following phrases with the preposition *i* should be noted: *i dag* (today), *i går* (yesterday), *i forgårs* (the day before yesterday), *i morgen* (to-morrow), *i overmorgen* (the day after to-morrow), *i morges* (this morning), *i formiddag* (this morning, before noon, before dinner time), *i ettermiddag* (this afternoon, after dinner time), *i aften* or *i kveld* (this evening, to-night), *i natt* (last night, this night), *i år* (this year), *i fjor* (last year), *i sommer* (last summer, this summer).

ifølge – "according to".

74

innen 1. "within": *innen en uke* (within a week); 2. "by", not later than: *innen klokken to* (by two o'clock).

med 1. "with", together with: *kom med meg* (come with me); 2. "by", by means of communication: *jeg reiste med toget* (I went by train), *beløpet ble betalt med sjekk* (the amount was paid by cheque).

mot or **imot** 1. "against": *vi kjempet mot en sterk fiende* (we fought against a strong enemy); 2. "towards": *Columbus seilte mot vest* (Columbus sailed towards west); 3. "to": *han er snill mot barna* (he is kind to the children).

om 1. "about": *vi har ikke hørt noe om ham* (we have not heard anything about him); 2. "in", "at", "on" (about a time or period when something usually happens): *om morgenen* (in the morning), *om formiddagen* (in the forenoon), *om ettermiddagen* (in the afternoon), *om dagen* (in the daytime), *om aftenen* (in the evening), *om søndagene* (on the Sundays), *om natten* (at night), *om sommeren* (in the summer); 3. "in" (about a period at the end of which something is going to happen): *om en time* (in an hour).
Note the following phrases with *om*, where the English have no prepositions: *tre ganger om året* (three times a year), *to timer om dagen* (two hours a day).

omkring – "about", "around".

ovenpå – "on", "on top of".

over 1. "over", "above": *de fløy over Nordpolen* (they flew over the North Pole); 2. "via": *reise over Bergen* (travel via Bergen); 3. "at": *overrasket over* (surprised at); 4. "of" (describing): *et kart over Oslo* (a map of Oslo), *en liste over prisene* (a list of the prices).

på 1. "on": *på bordet* (on the table); 2. "in", "at" (in many place-names with *øy* [island], *berg* or *fjell* [mountain] and inland towns): *på De Britiske Øyer* (in the British Isles), *på Cuba* (in Cuba), *på Bygdøy* (at Bygdöy), *på Ekeberg* (at Ekeberg), *på Lillehammer* (at Lillehammer).
Note: *på skolen* (at school), *gå på skolen* (go to school), *gå på kino* (go to the movies), *høre på* (listen to), *vente på* (wait for).

siden – "since".

til 1. "to" (about a place): *velkommen til Norge* (welcome to Norway); 2. "till" (about time in affirmative expressions; cf. *før*): *vent til i morgen* (wait till to-morrow); 3. "for" (meant for): *her er et brev til Dem* (here is a letter for you), *vi skal ha fisk til middag* (we shall have fish for dinner); 4. "in": *til tross for* (in spite of).

In Old Norse *til* governed the genitive case, which is still preserved in some phrases (see above § 30).

under 1. "under", "below", "beneath"; 2. "during", in the course of: *under den annen verdenskrig* (during the second world war).

unntagen – "except".

uten – "without".

utenfor – "outside".

ved 1. "at" (near); 2. "by" (by the help of).

§ 151. In Norwegian prepositions can govern infinitives where English must apply the gerund ing-form of the verb: *jeg er trett av å lese* (I am tired of reading), *han er interessert i å høre nytt fra oss* (he is interested in hearing news from us), *hun var ergerlig over å ha mistet vesken sin* (she was annoyed at having lost her bag), *han gikk uten å si et ord* (he left without saying a word).

§ 152. Prepositions can also be placed in front of a that-clause where they are omitted in English or a supporting "it" or "the fact" is added: *jeg er redd for at prisene vil stige* (I am afraid that prices will rise), *hun var skuffet over at ingen husket hennes fødselsdag* (she was disappointed that nobody remembered her birthday), *vi er vant til at han kommer sent hjem* (we are accustomed to it [the fact] that he comes home late.)

Word Order *(Ordstilling)*

§ 153. The regular word order in both principal and subordinate clauses is: subject + predicate:

bussen kommer (the bus comes, the bus is coming)
jeg vet når bussen kommer (I know when the bus comes, when the bus will come)

subject + predicate + object:

han kjøpte billett (he bought a ticket)
hun så at han kjøpte billett (she saw that he bought a ticket)

subject + predicate + indirect object + object:

mange skylder min far penger (many people owe my father money)
du vet at mange skylder min far penger (you know that many people owe my father money)

subject + predicate + indirect object + object + prepositional phrase:

han brakte meg en bok fra sin bror (he brought me a book from his brother)
jeg ble glad da han brakte meg en bok fra sin bror (I was glad when he brought me a book from his brother)

INVERSION *(Inversjon)*

§ 154. In some cases the subject comes after the predicate in **principal clauses** while the other parts preserve the above word order.

a) **Interrogative sentences** are formed by placing the predicate before the subject. There is no equivalent to the English transcription with the verb "do":

stopper bussen her? (does the bus stop here?)
kjøpte han billett? (did he buy a ticket?)
skylder mange min far penger? (do many people owe my father money?)
brakte han meg en bok fra sin bror? (did he bring me a book from his brother?)

When the predicate in an interrogative sentence is composed of principal and auxiliary verbs, the subject comes after the auxiliary but before the principal verb:

har bussen kommet? (has the bus arrived?)
kan han kjøpe billett? (can he buy a ticket?)

There is no inversion when the subject is an interrogative pronoun or if the noun or pronoun used as subject is preceded by an interrogative pronoun or adverb:

hvem kommer? (who comes? who is coming?)
hvilken buss kommer? (which bus comes? which bus is coming?)
hvor mange skylder min far penger? (how many people owe my father money?)

b) **Affirmative clauses** have inversion of subject and predicate when they are preceded by subordinate clauses; compare the following sentences:

han solgte bilen da krigen brøt ut   da krigen brøt ut, *solgte han* bilen
(he sold the car when the war   (when the war broke out, he sold
broke out)   the car)

jeg tar en drosje hvis det regner   hvis det regner, *tar jeg* en drosje
(I take a taxi if it rains)   (if it rains, I take a taxi)

jeg skal bo på hotell når jeg   når jeg kommer til byen, *skal jeg*
kommer til byen (I shall live   bo på hotell (when I come to town,
at a hotel when I come to town)   I shall live at a hotel)

c) Inversion also occurs when, for emphasis, the sentence begins with the object, the indirect object, a predicative noun or a predicative adjective:

denne bilen **kjøpte jeg** *i London* (this car I bought in London)
fedrelandet **skylder vi** *alt* (to our country we owe everything)
forræder **har han** *ikke vært* (a traitor he has not been)
forferdelig **er det** (terrible it is)

d) Likewise when the sentence begins with an emphatic adverb or with an adverbial expression. Compare the following sentences:

bussen kommer klokken to (the   klokken to *kommer bussen* (at
bus arrives at two o'clock)   two o'clock the bus arrives)

han kjøpte billett der (he   der *kjøpte han* billett
bought a ticket there)   (there he bought a ticket)

hun har levert konduktøren   nå *har hun* levert konduktøren sin
sin billett nå (she has   billett (now she has handed
handed the conductor her   the conductor her ticket)
ticket now)

det var kaldt i vinter   i vinter *var det* kaldt (this
(it was cold this winter)   winter it was cold)

Note: A conjunction (§ 110) does not change the word order: *han reiste til Oslo, og han studerte ved Universitetet i seks år* (he went to Oslo, and he studied at the University for six years); *men ingen vet hvor de bor* (but nobody knows where they live)

e) Inversion takes place in a principal clause after a direct quotation or part of a direct quotation:

«Kan du si meg hvor gammel han er?» **spurte hun** ("Can you tell me how old he is?" she asked)

«Jeg tror han er førti år,» **svarte jeg** ("I think he is forty years old," I answered)

«Overalt,» **sa professoren** *«kan man finne spor av denne kultur»* ("Everywhere," said the professor, "one can find traces of this culture")

f) Inversion may be used in subjunctive clauses expressing a wish:

> *komme ditt rike!* (thy kingdom come!)
> *leve Kongen!* (long live the King!)

But the uninverted word order is just as usual:

> *ditt rike komme!*
> *Kongen leve!*

§ 155. **Subordinate clauses have usually the uninverted word order.** The only exception is conditional clauses where the conjunction is left out (see § 111 c). Compare the following sentences:

Hvis **du kommer** *med toget, skal jeg møte deg på stasjonen* (if you come by train, I shall meet you at the station)

Kommer du *med toget, skal jeg møte deg på stasjonen* (if you come by train, I shall meet you at the station)

POSITION OF ADVERBS *(Adverbers stilling)*

§ 156. An adverb modifying an adjective (and participles) is placed before it, as in English:

en meget gammel dame (a very old lady)
en svært opptatt mann (a very busy man)
en kraftig bygd gutt (a strongly built boy)
en langsomt svinnende tone (a slowly fading tone)

§ 157. An interrogative adverb is, as in English, placed in front of both principal and subordinate clauses:

hvor bor han? (where does he live?)
hvor gammel er Deres søster? (how old is your sister?)
hvorledes hendte dette? (how did this happen?)
jeg vet ikke hvor han bor (I do not know where he lives)
han kan si meg hvor gammel Deres søster er (he can tell me how old your sister is)
ingen vet hvorledes dette hendte (nobody knows how this happened)

§ 158. In principal clauses all other adverbs are usually placed after the verb (predicate):

gutten synger godt (the boy sings well)
jeg bor alltid på dette hotellet (I always stay at this hotel)
hun åpnet plutselig døren (she suddenly opened the door)
ingen bor her (nobody lives here)
kjør aldri mot rødt lys (never drive through a red light)
hun gråt bittert (she cried bitterly)
disse plantene gror overalt (these plants grow everywhere)

§ 159. In compound tenses the adverb is placed after the past participle or the infinitive:

gutten har sunget godt (the boy has sung well)
hun hadde grått bittert (she had cried bitterly)
vi kan ikke vente lenge (we cannot wait long)
ingen kan bo her (nobody can live here)

(For the position of the negative adverb *ikke* (not) and some other adverbs denoting time, see §§ 161–165).

§ 160. The same word order is preserved also in subordinate clauses:

la meg få vite om gutten synger godt (let me know whether the boy sings well)
de sier at hun gråt bittert (they say that she wept bitterly)
det er kunngjort at ingen må bo her (it has been announced that nobody must live here)
jeg ble interessert fordi disse plantene kan gro overalt (I became interested because these plants can grow everywhere)

(For the position of the negative adverb *ikke* (not) and some other adverbs denoting time, see §§ 161–165.)

NEGATION AND THE PLACE OF THE NEGATIVE ADVERB *ikke*

§ 161. Norwegian has no equivalent to the English transcription with the verb "do" in negative sentences. The negation is expressed by means of the negative adverb *ikke* (not), as it is often done also in Shakespearean language:

"I know not why I am so sad" *(jeg vet ikke hvorfor jeg er så trist)*.

§ 162. The negative adverb *ikke* is placed immediately after the verb in a **principal clause**. If, however, there is a personal pronoun as object, the *ikke* comes after it, and if there is a personal pronoun as indirect object, the *ikke* is placed after that. In compound tenses *ikke* stands between the auxiliary and the principal verb.

bussen kommer ikke (the bus does not come, is not coming)
han kjøpte ikke billett til henne (he did not buy a ticket for her)
mannen kjøpte ikke billett til henne (the man did not buy a ticket for her)
hun leverte ikke konduktøren sin billett (she did not hand the conductor her ticket)
jeg ser ham ikke (I do not see him)
hun leverte ham ikke sin billett (she did not hand him her ticket)
toget har ikke kommet (the train has not arrived)
jeg har ikke vært i Amerika på mange år (I have not been in America for many years)
min bror vil ikke selge bilen sin (my brother will not sell his car)

§ 163. The noun-subject of a negative question is usually placed immediately after *ikke;* but the pronoun-subject is placed immediately after the verb, and the other parts of the clause come in the same succession as shown in § 162.

kommer ikke bussen? (does not the bus come? is not the bus coming?)
vil ikke din bror selge bilen sin? (won't your brother sell his car?)
har ikke toget kommet? (hasn't the train arrived?)
kjøpte ikke mannen billett til henne? (didn't the man buy a ticket for her?)
kjøpte han ikke billett? (did he not buy a ticket?)
leverte hun ham ikke sin billett? (did she not hand him her ticket?)
leverte hun ikke konduktøren sin billett? (did she not hand the conductor her ticket?)
har de ikke vært i Amerika på mange år? (have they not been in America for many years?)

§ 164. In **subordinate clauses** the *ikke* is placed before the verb (predicate):
vi er redd for at bussen ikke kommer (we are afraid that the bus will not come)

han beklaget at han ikke hadde kjøpt billett til henne (he regretted that he had not bought a ticket for her)
når jeg ikke ser ham, blir jeg nervøs (when I do not see him, I become nervous)

siden de ikke har vært i Amerika, vil de gjerne lese noen bøker om landet (since they have not been in America, they would like to read some books about the country)

§ 165. What has been said about the *ikke*, as far as word order is concerned, applies also to some other adverbs denoting time: *alltid* or *bestandig* (always), *ofte* (often), *sjelden* (seldom), *gjerne* (usually), *aldri* (never):

han kjøpte alltid billett (he always bought a ticket)
jeg har ofte vært i Amerika (I have often been in America)
kjøpte han gjerne billett? (did he usually buy a ticket?)
siden de aldri har vært i Amerika, vil de kjøpe noen bøker om landet (since they have never been in America, they want to buy some books about the country).

Interjections

§ 166 Interjections are words of exclamation that can be used to render onomatopoeia (sound-imitating words) e.g. **mø** (for a cow), **nøff** (for a pig), **vovv** (for a dog), **kykkeliky** (for a rooster), but also to express feelings and moods, such as **au** (about a pain), **isj** or **esj** (to describe arrogance or repulsion), **fy** (about disgust).

§ 167 Interjections can also include the answer words **ja** (yes) and **nei** (no). Note, however, that while *ja* is an affirmative answer to a positive question e.g. *Kommer De i kveld?* (Are you coming tonight?) **jo** (yes) is an affirmative answer to a negative question e.g. *Kommer De ikke i kveld? Jo.* (Are you not coming tonight? Yes.)